STUDENT FOOD

IN COLOUR

CATHERINE ATKINSON

foulsham

LONDON • NEW YORK • TORONTO • SYDNEY

foulsham

The Publishing House, Bennetts Close, Cippenham,
Slough, Berkshire, SL1 5AP, England

Foulsham books can be found in all good bookshops and direct from
www.foulsham.com

ISBN: 978-0-572-03365-1

Copyright © 2007 The National Magazine Company Limited

Cover photograph © Superstock

A CIP record for this book is available from the British Library

The moral right of the author has been asserted

Printed in Dubai

Contents

Introduction

Are you leaving home for the first time and fending for yourself? It may come as a shock when you no longer have the luxury of a hot cooked meal waiting for you when you get home at the end of the day. Worse than that, not only will you have to shop for and prepare your own food, you will have to do it on a meagre budget. Don't despair! Even when money is tight, eating to stay mentally and physically alert need not be a problem – you can still eat nutritionally and enjoyably.

Top tips
on getting started

Getting started
- Getting started has never been easier. In this book you'll find all the information you need – from store cupboard and equipment essentials to basic cooking skills that take you beyond opening the customary can of baked beans.

Easy on numbers
- Most recipes in this book serve four, which is ideal if you share a house and all cook together. This is the cheapest way of getting fed and the easiest – it takes only a little longer to prepare food for four than it does for one, and you won't have to do the cooking every day. If you are cooking just for yourself, though – or for two or more – the recipes are designed to be easy to adapt.

Simple to use
- The recipes are simply set out so that you can see how long each one should take to prepare and cook and what ingredients you will need to buy. These are the perfect recipes for amateur cooks to try and then turn to again and again.

Kitchen kit

While your student accommodation may have a ready-equipped kitchen, it's just as likely that you'll be starting from scratch and will need to provide your own cooking utensils. Check out what's been provided, then persuade someone (your parents being the obvious first candidates) to give or lend you the rest. There's no need to go overboard – start with the basics and you can easily add one or two extra items as and when you need them. Unused gadgets are just a nuisance that get in the way or collect dust!

Top tips
on what you need

Absolute essentials
- Bottle opener
- Can opener – not all cans have ring-pull tops
- Small sharp knife, and a bigger one if you can afford it, plus a bread knife with a serrated edge
- Large non-stick frying pan – it's worth buying a new good-quality one
- Saucepans with lids – ideally one large for cooking pasta, rice and soups and a smaller one
- Wooden spoon and spatula
- Grater
- Colander or large sieve (strainer)
- Mixing bowl that can double up as a serving bowl
- Chopping board – a plastic one is easier to keep clean and germ-free
- Cutlery, plates, bowls, mugs and glasses
- Tea towels (dish cloths) and oven gloves

Really useful things
- Measuring spoons and jug or measuring cups – they take the guesswork out of cooking
- Kettle – much faster than boiling water in a saucepan
- Toaster – easier than standing over the grill
- Fish slice – for lifting food out of pans and for serving

6

- Roasting tin – if it's old, line it with foil when using
- Baking (cookie) sheet or tray – for everything from oven chips (fries) to pizzas
- Potato masher
- Corkscrew – or buy screw-top bottles!
- Flameproof casserole dish (Dutch oven) – these can be used on both the hob and oven, but an ovenproof one is okay – and baking dishes

Great for keen cooks

- Hand-held blender for smooth soups, sauces and dips
- Pepper mill plus a supply of black peppercorns
- Wok – great for stir-fries
- Garlic crusher – if you get fed up with chopping garlic or crushing it on a board with the back of a spoon
- Potato peeler
- Weighing scales – if you want to be really accurate

Stocking up before you start

Invest in a few basics at the beginning of term (a kind relative may help you out) and you'll have a few standbys to rustle up meals in minutes. Buying everything on this list between you won't cost a fortune and some items will last you all year. As a guide, buy large or bulk quantities of items you use often, such a tea bags, and small amounts of things you only use occasionally, like dried herbs. Or if you think you'll never use them, don't buy them at all!

Top tips
on what to keep in the cupboard

A dozen store cupboard essentials

- Oil – vegetable or sunflower oil is fine for most dishes
- Tinned tomatoes – whole ones are cheaper than chopped ones
- Dried pasta, rice and couscous
- Flavourings – salt and pepper and dried mixed herbs
- Red or white wine vinegar – for salad dressings and marinades
- Stock cubes or bouillon powder – if you can only afford one type, vegetable stock can be used in all dishes
- Cornflour (cornstarch) – for thickening sauces and casseroles
- Baked beans and a couple of cans of pulses such as red kidney beans or chick peas (economy brands are fine) and vegetables such as sweetcorn
- Tins of fish such as tuna (check the label for 'dolphin friendly') and sardines
- Canned fruit – try economy peach slices and fruit cocktail, which are great for an impromptu dessert or snack, and canned pineapple is often used in cooking
- Table sauces – ketchup (catsup), soy sauce, mustard, mayonnaise
- Tea bags and coffee

Important perishables

- Bread (wholemeal is better for you and more filling) and pitta breads, which usually last for a month or two in the unopened pack so are a good standby
- Onions and garlic
- Potatoes (keep them in a cool dark place to stop them going green/sprouting)
- Favourite fresh fruits such as apples, oranges and bananas (don't store bananas in the fridge because they'll go brown)

Fresh in the fridge

- Butter or margarine (choose one that can be used for both spreading and cooking)
- Fresh milk
- Cheese – medium or mature adds more flavour than mild, so you'll need less
- Eggs
- Fresh lemons or bottled lemon juice – for salad dressings and jazzing up sauces
- Vegetables, especially carrots, mushrooms, (bell) peppers and salad stuff
- Tube of tomato purée (paste)

Freezer foods

- Meat including chicken breasts, minced (ground) beef and sausages (defrost in the fridge overnight)
- Vegetables such as peas and sweetcorn
- Loaf or half-loaf of sliced bread (toast from frozen if necessary)
- Plastic carton of milk (for when you run out of fresh) – allow to defrost in the fridge for several hours, then give it a good shake before using

Tip

- For food storage, use a clean and dry cupboard that is in the coolest part of your kitchen, not next to the oven, boiler or radiator. Pack the shelves logically, with similar foods next to each other (so that you can see exactly what you've got and avoid buying duplicates) and items you use most often at the front.

Don't waste your time — or your money

As a student, you will probably have a limited food budget. Don't despair; there are ways to make your money stretch a long way without resorting to beans on toast – again! In between rushing to lectures, writing essays and your busy social life, try to find 5 minutes to plan the meals you're going to eat in the coming week. This may sound tedious, but in the long run can save you umpteen dashes to the campus supermarket and stop food growing mould in the fridge because you'd forgotten you were going home for the weekend.

Work out how much you can afford to spend on food each week and stick to it. Otherwise you'll find yourself eating ready-made gourmet meals at the start of term and recycling tea bags by the end.

Top tips to make your money go further

When shopping

Make a list
- Before you set out, make a shopping list – but prepare to be flexible. For example, a beef stir-fry can easily be changed to a chicken stir-fry if chicken breasts are a better buy.

Buy at markets
- Market stalls are cheaper than the supermarket for fresh produce – but check the quality and don't be cajoled into buying more than you need; a big bag of avocadoes won't be a bargain if you can only manage to eat a couple before the rest go bad.

Bag a bargain
- Go to the supermarket at the end of the day, or on Sunday afternoons when fresh produce nearing its sell-by date is sold at a reduced price.

Buy in season
- Choose fruit and vegetables that are in season. It stands to reason that in the winter you'll pay a lot more for summer produce that has to be flown from a warmer part of the globe.

Try own brands
- Many supermarkets now offer 'value' products such as bread, pasta, tinned tomatoes, cheese and long-life milk. These are a

fraction of the price of branded goods, but remember that some economy products such as sausages will contain less meat and more rusk filler and fat, so may not be such a good buy.

Buy loose

- When shopping at the supermarket, buy loose fruit and vegetables rather than pre-packed. You can save money by simply picking up a bag and filling it yourself. This also allows you to select the best quality and the exact quantity you want.

Use frozen

- Frozen vegetables and tins of fruit and vegetables are good alternatives to fresh. They also keep for ages and will probably still be 'in-date' when you've left college!

Snap up special offers

- Take advantage of special offers such as 'buy-one-get-one-free' or '30% extra'. This is great for essentials, but don't be seduced into buying things you don't really want.

When cooking

Back to basics

- Get back to basics – processed food is an expensive option because you are paying for the preparation. It's much cheaper (and usually healthier) to buy the basics and make your own meals. Why pay for a bottle of curry sauce when you can spend the same amount on a jar of curry paste, which will flavour a dozen dinners?

Don't forget fillers

- Base meals around starchy foods such as bread, rice, pasta and potatoes and use beans, peas and lentils as a cheap source of protein to bulk out casseroles and similar dishes instead of meat.

Go for flavour

- Cook with well-flavoured ingredients and you'll need to use less of them. For example, you will need less Cheddar when making a sauce if you buy mature rather than mild.

Cook and freeze

- Buying a separate set of ingredients for every meal can work out expensive so, where possible, cook double quantities and pop half in the freezer for another day. (Let it defrost overnight in the fridge, so that it's ready to cook when you get back from lectures.) This is a brilliant time saver for those really busy days.

Double up in the oven

- If you're paying the fuel bill, make the most of your oven. When roasting meat, for example, do jacket potatoes and braised vegetables at the same time.

Watch your waste

- Use produce such as fresh fruit and vegetables and raw meat in meals at the beginning of the week when they are at their best, and frozen and canned foods for later meals.

Keep it clean!

You may think that having piles of unwashed dishes and eating up leftover takeaways is part of student life, but a bout of food poisoning will do nothing for your studies or social life.

Don't risk it – you may economise when buying food, but when it comes to hygiene you can't afford to cut corners.

Get into the habit of clearing up and washing up as soon as you've finished eating, and make sure everyone does their fair share!

Top tips on food hygiene

Wash your hands

- Don't spread germs – always wash your hands thoroughly before and after cooking, especially after touching raw meat and fish. Wipe work surfaces before you start with a clean cloth washed in hot soapy water. Invest in an anti-bacterial spray – especially if other members of your household have dubious hygiene habits.

Separate raw and cooked

- Don't store raw and cooked meat close together in the fridge; keep them separate and covered. Raw meat is best kept on the bottom shelf so that it can't drip over any other foods.

Don't overfill the fridge or it will run too warm and the cold air won't be able to circulate properly.

Freeze immediately

- If you buy food for freezing, make sure you do this as soon as you return from shopping. Don't re-freeze raw foods that have defrosted unless you cook them first.

Watch the dates

- 'Use-by' dates mean exactly what they say. Once the date has passed, you can't be sure that the food is safe to eat – it belongs in the bin. If the pack says 'eat within 3 days' there's a reason for it (such as E.coli or salmonella!). 'Best before' dates are used on less perishable foods such as dried pasta or biscuits. The food may not taste as good, but will still be safe to eat a few weeks after the date has gone.

Throw out anything mouldy

- When you spot signs of mould on food, don't be tempted to cut off the mouldy bit and eat the rest. Moulds and fungi have invisible toxins that can penetrate the entire food. Throw it away.

Store sensibly

- Always transfer leftovers to a clean container or plate and cover with a lid, clingfilm (plastic wrap) or foil. Cool quickly before storing and never put warm food in the fridge. If you want to freeze leftovers to eat at another time, make sure they are well wrapped and label the pack (all lumps of frozen foods look the same). As a rough guide, most cooked foods will freeze for 4–6 months. Don't try to freeze eggs, foods with mayonnaise or single (light) cream, potatoes or bananas.

Reheat to piping hot

- When reheating food, always make sure it is piping hot throughout so that any bugs are killed off. Never reheat previously cooked food more than once.

Wash up!

- Wash up with hot water – if there's none in the tank, boil a kettle and mix with cold. Use a clean tea towel (dish cloth) when drying up; dirty ones can be a breeding ground for bacteria. Otherwise, let the dishes air-dry.

Tidy up as you go

- Finally, try to keep the kitchen clean and tidy – this may sound like the nagging you left home to avoid, but tidying up as you go along really is good kitchen commonsense. There's nothing worse than tackling dishes that have been festering for several days, or not being able to find a clean coffee mug. Remember that in the right conditions one bacterium could multiply to thousands of millions in just 12 hours.

Kitchen basics

Cooking a meal is no big deal! Simply decide what you are going to cook, make sure you have all the equipment you need, collect the ingredients together, cook, eat and wash up. Be confident and don't panic if the food doesn't turn out quite how you had hoped. Most likely it will taste great but, if not, you'll be able to improve it next time. The key to cooking is mastering some basic techniques and knowing the answers to just a few questions. Here's the basics to get you started.

Top tips for new cooks

How big are a tablespoon and a teaspoon?

- Use proper measuring spoons (a teaspoon holds 5 ml and a tablespoon 15 ml) – plastic ones are really cheap. You can make do with an ordinary teaspoon and tablespoon (this is slightly larger than a dessertspoon, the one you use for puddings). When measuring dry ingredients, they should always be levelled on the spoon, unless the recipe says otherwise.

Does it matter which oil I use?

- You can use sunflower or any good-quality oil in any of these recipes. A few say olive oil is preferable, but this isn't essential. Avoid really cheap vegetable oils; they will spoil the flavour of your food.

What if I don't have all the right ingredients?

- Don't start cooking until you've read the recipe and checked you have the essential ingredients to make it work. Next, be creative and don't be scared to adapt the recipes. Try different types of meat or vegetables – and add your favourite herbs and spices. Your experiments may not always be as successful as you had hoped, but you could be a chef in the making.

What's the difference between boil and simmer?

- Boiling is when the cooking liquid bubbles rapidly at a temperature of at least 100°C/212°F and is great for cooking foods such as rice as it helps to keep the grains separate. When you simmer, the heat is turned down a little so the liquid bubbles gently; this is perfect for casseroles and stews as it will help tenderise the meat.

How can I fry food and make sure it's crisp?

- Always heat the oil first otherwise the cold oil will soak into the food and make it soggy. The oil should be hot but not smoking (or the food may burn and you could set the pan on fire!). Test this by holding your hand about 4 cm/ 2 in above the pan (but not with dangly sleeves!); it should feel hot, but not uncomfortable. Alternatively, add a scrap of the food or a small piece of bread to the pan – it should start to sizzle straight away.

Why do I burn everything before it's cooked through?

- The temperature is too high, so the outside of the food is browning before the middle has started to cook. If you're frying, brown one side of the food, turn it over, then turn down the heat and finish cooking. If food is burning in the oven, it's likely that your oven is over-heating; in future set it to a slightly lower temperature. You could also have put the dish too near the top so, unless a recipe says otherwise, use the middle shelf of the oven. If you're using a fan oven it will cook more quickly, so

use the lower temperature given in the recipes.

Can I leave meat rare?

- Beef, lamb and duck can all be served 'rare'. To test if a steak or chop is cooked to your liking, press on it when browned on both sides. If it feels very spongy, it will be rare; if firmer, but still with a bit of 'give', it will be medium; if firm, it will be well done. You can give it a final test with a fork or knife to see if the juices that run out are pink (rare/medium) or clear (well done), but don't do this too often or the meat will be dry. Pork (including sausages), chicken and turkey should always be thoroughly cooked and never even the slightest bit pink.

How do I tell when a food is cooked?

- With a knife! If you're cooking something like meatballs or fish fingers, cut it in half to check it's cooked through. For a lasagne or fish pie, put a knife into the middle – it will slide in easily if the dish is cooked and when removed should still be scorching hot.

What if part of the meal is cooked before the rest?

- Put it on a warm plate, cover with foil and leave in a warm place, such as the oven set to the lowest temperature. Pasta and rice will be fine for a few minutes left in a colander over the sink with a lid on top. A hot gravy or sauce poured over just before serving can also work wonders.

Keep it simple

The recipes in this book provide fast and nutritious food whether you have done a bit of cooking before or are just starting out in the kitchen.

Some of the dishes are complete meals in themselves, others have serving suggestions such as rice or potatoes. If you're baffled about how to cook these, here are some of the basics. Once you gain confidence, you'll be mixing and matching to make your own meals.

Top tips
on cooking the basics

Boiling rice

- Rice can be prepared in many ways, including oven-baked (see page 66), but the easiest way is to boil it. Some varieties need to be rinsed or soaked first, so check the instructions on the pack. To accompany a main meal, allow 75 g/3 oz/⅓ cup per person. Long-grain American rice may be the cheapest, but 'easy-cook' gives great results every time; the rice is pre-treated so the grains always stay separate.

- To boil rice in lots of water, half-fill a large pan with water and add a pinch of salt. Heat the water until it boils rapidly, then add the rice and bring it back to the boil. Turn down the heat a little and cook the rice for as long as it says on the pack (usually 10–12 minutes). Test it by removing a few grains; it should be just tender. Drain the rice through a large sieve (strainer) or fine-holed colander. If it looks a bit 'sticky', pour a kettleful of boiling water over it, drain again and stir gently with a fork to loosen and fluff up the grains.

- To cook rice in a measured amount of water (or stock, which gives it a wonderful flavour), measure the rice in a cup, then add exactly double that amount of water or stock. Heat them both in the pan to boiling point, stir once, then turn down the heat a little. Cover the pan with a tight-fitting lid. Cook the rice for as long as it says on the pack. If any liquid is left, heat the pan without the lid for another minute.

Cooking pasta or noodles

- Pasta is cooked in much the same way as rice, but always in plenty of boiling water. Allow about 100 g/4 oz/1 cup of small to medium pasta shapes per person. Use the biggest possible pan, half-fill it with water, then add a pinch of salt and about 5 ml/1 tsp of oil (this stops the pasta sticking together). Pour in the pasta, give it a stir, then bring the water back to the boil. Turn down the heat just a little until the water is still boiling but not too fiercely. Don't cover the pan, or it will boil over. Pasta usually takes 8–10 minutes to cook; wholemeal pasta takes a little longer. Test by removing a piece with a wooden spoon, then running it under the cold tap to cool a bit before tasting. It should be tender but still firm.

Cooking jacket potatoes

- Jacket potatoes are a great accompaniment but also make a nutritious meal on their own when topped with grated cheese, flaked tuna or baked beans. To oven-bake them, heat your oven to 180°C/350°F/gas 4/fan oven 160°C. Scrub some big potatoes with a brush to remove any dirt and prick the skins with a fork (this stops them exploding in the oven!). Bake on a baking tray, or directly on the oven shelf for 1¼–1½ hours.

Check they're cooked by pushing the point of a sharp knife into the middle – it should go in really easily. You can speed up baking by pushing a metal skewer through the raw potato (this conducts heat to the middle) before putting it in the oven.

- You can also cook jacket potatoes in a microwave. Prick the skin in several places with a sharp knife or fork (again, essential). For a 225 g/8 oz potato, microwave on high for 4 minutes, then rub the skin with a little oil and salt, if liked – but carefully because it will be hot. Microwave for a further 1–2 minutes or until the potato feels soft when gently squeezed. Leave to 'rest' for a couple of minutes before serving. Adding more potatoes to the microwave will slow down cooking time; two will take about 7 minutes and four about 10 minutes. You'll have to keep checking though, as microwaves differ hugely and overcooked microwaved potatoes will be shrivelled and tough.

Boiling potatoes and root vegetables

- To prepare and boil potatoes and root vegetables such as carrots, peel thinly or scrape or scrub as necessary, then cut into even-sized pieces (slices or sticks for carrots, large chunks for potatoes). Leave small new potatoes and baby carrots whole. Put in a saucepan with just enough cold water to cover and add a pinch of salt if liked. Bring to the boil, then turn down the heat to moderate, cover the pan and simmer until the vegetables feel tender when pierced with the point of a knife (5–20 minutes depending on the vegetable and size of the pieces). Tip into a colander to drain (you could save the vegetable water for gravy or soup).

Boiling green vegetables

- For vegetables such as mangetout (snow peas), green beans and broccoli, rinse them under cold water (to remove any dirt or dust) and trim them as necessary, then place in a saucepan. Pour over enough boiling water from the kettle to just cover them, then bring back to the boil, reduce the heat a little, cover and simmer until tender (2–3 minutes for mangetout, 4–5 for green beans and 5–6 for broccoli). Drain in a colander. If you don't have a kettle, bring the water to the boil in a saucepan, then add the vegetables.

Making an omelette

- To make an omelette to serve one, whisk 2 eggs with 15 ml/ 1 tbsp of water, some chopped fresh herbs, if liked, and a little salt and pepper. Heat an 18 cm/ 7 in non-stick frying pan, add 15 g/½ oz/1 tbsp of butter or sunflower margarine and swirl it around the pan as it melts. Pour in the egg and cook for about 1 minute, stirring gently with a wooden spatula. When the egg starts to set, stop stirring and cook for a further minute, or until the underside is golden brown and the top is just set. Scatter some grated cheese or cooked mushrooms down the middle

then, using the spatula, fold in the two sides. Slide the folded omelette on to a plate and serve straight away.

Cooking sausages

- To cook sausages, cut the links with kitchen scissors or a sharp knife. Put them in a dry non-stick pan over a moderate heat (don't prick them first or you'll loose precious juices) and cook for about 5 minutes, turning frequently until they start to brown and give out a little fat. Lower the heat and cook for a further 12–15 minutes or until well browned all over and cooked through. Never cook sausages at a high temperature or they may burst and the middles may still be raw when the outside has browned. You can also cook sausages under a medium grill (broiler) – line the grill pan with foil first – for 10–15 minutes, turning frequently, or bake them at 180°C/350°F/gas 4/fan oven 160°C for about 30 minutes, turning and basting a few times.

Roasting chicken

- To cook a whole chicken, make sure a frozen one is thoroughly defrosted first and remove any giblets (in a plastic bag inside the chicken – most 'oven-ready' chickens are sold without). Check the weight on the pack and calculate the cooking time, allowing 20 minutes per 450 g/ 1 lb, plus a further 20 minutes. Put half a lemon and a few fresh herbs in the cavity for flavour, if you like, season with salt and pepper and smear the breast with butter or oil or cover with a few rashers (slices) of fatty bacon (or you can just cut off and use the fatty bit and rind of some back bacon and save the lean part). Put in a roasting tin, preferably on a roasting rack as this allows heat to circulate, and cook for the calculated time, basting with the juices occasionally.

- Check towards the end of the cooking time; if the breast is starting to over-brown, remove the chicken from the oven, cover with a 'tent' of foil, then put it back in the oven. The chicken is cooked when the juices run clear when the flesh is pierced with a knife between the body and a leg. Take the chicken out of the oven, cover it with a large sheet of foil and leave it to 'rest' for about 10 minutes before carving (this lets all the juices settle and makes it easier to slice or cut into pieces).

Roasting chicken portions

- If you don't want to roast a whole chicken, buy portions instead. Leave the skins on to keep the meat moist (you can remove them after cooking if preferred). Place them on a rack in a foil-lined roasting tin, sprinkle with salt and pepper and roast at 190ºC/375ºF/gas 5/fan oven 170ºC for about 35 minutes or until tender and thoroughly cooked.

Cooking bacon

- The key to cooking bacon is to get the grill (broiler) or frying pan hot to start with, so that the bacon sizzles and quickly becomes crisp. Pre-heat the grill to high and, while you're waiting, line the grill pan with foil (this saves on washing up) and arrange the bacon in a single layer on the wire rack. If you prefer, cut off the rind and a little of the fat with kitchen scissors first. Grill for about 5 minutes if you like it lightly cooked and for about 7 minutes if you prefer it crispy. Turn it over half-way through cooking. Don't walk away and leave it cooking; it can burn very quickly. If you want to fry the bacon, use a large non-stick frying pan. Heat the pan over a high heat for about a minute, then add the bacon and cook as before.

Making a salad

- Pretty much anything goes here – lettuce, onions, (bell) peppers, courgettes (zucchini), spring onions (scallions), cucumber. Use what you have or what's on special offer. Wash it, then shred, slice, chop or tear it into pieces and toss it together with a little dressing if you like (see page 22).

Poultry

Lean, healthy and versatile, try quarters, breast fillets and the more economical thighs and drumsticks. Look out for goujons too, ideal for stir-frying and curries and coating in egg and breadcrumbs to shallow-fry. Try minced (ground) chicken instead of beef or lamb. Check the use-by date and make sure the meat looks really fresh, then get it into a fridge asap, well wrapped. Wash your hands before and after handling and never use the same utensils for preparing raw poultry and cooked foods. Frozen poultry will keep for up to 3 months; defrost in the fridge for 24 hours. Cook poultry thoroughly: to check, pierce the flesh at the thickest point; the juices should run clear and not be at all pink.

Garlic chicken with broccoli

> **Serves 4**
> **Ready in 15 minutes**

350 g/12 oz dried tagliatelle

225 g/8 oz broccoli, cut into florets

45 ml/3 tbsp oil, preferably olive

2 garlic cloves, peeled and finely chopped or crushed

Juice of ½ lemon or 30 ml/ 2 tbsp bottled lemon juice

30 ml/2 tbsp raisins

3 cooked chicken breasts or 400 g/14 oz thickly sliced cooked chicken, cut into strips

Salt and freshly ground black pepper

1 Cook the pasta in a large pan of lightly salted boiling water for 8–10 minutes or according to the packet instructions, adding the broccoli for the last 4 minutes of cooking time.

2 Meanwhile, heat the oil and garlic gently in a saucepan for 2 minutes. Add the lemon juice, raisins and chicken and heat gently for a further 3 minutes.

3 Drain the pasta and broccoli into a colander, then return to the hot pan. Add the chicken mixture and gently toss together. Season to taste, divide between warm serving plates and serve straight away.

Tips

- Dried fruit is a good source of iron, a lack of which can make you feel tired. You don't have to buy a huge bag as it also comes in handy little 'lunchbox-sized' packs. Sultanas (golden raisins) or 8 chopped dried apricots can be used instead of the raisins in this recipe, if you prefer.

- If you prefer to cook your own chicken breasts, follow the method on page 19.

Garlic chicken with broccoli

Lemon and herb chicken

Serves 4
Ready in 15 minutes

4 large skinless, boneless
chicken breasts
or 8 chicken drumsticks

15 ml/1 tbsp oil

Finely grated rind and juice
of 1 lemon

10 ml/2 tsp dried mixed herbs

Salt and freshly ground
black pepper

200 g/7 oz bag of mixed
salad leaves

30 ml/2 tbsp French
dressing

1 Make two or three shallow slashes on each chicken breast or through the skin of each drumstick with a sharp knife. Put in a non-metallic dish, large enough to hold them in a single layer.

2 Mix together the oil, lemon rind and juice and herbs. Spoon over the chicken and turn to coat thoroughly. Season with salt and pepper.

3 Preheat the grill to medium-high, place the prepared chicken on a foil-lined grill rack and cook chicken breasts for 5–6 minutes on each side or drumsticks for 12–15 minutes, turning several times, or until cooked through and tender.

4 While the chicken is cooking, toss the salad leaves with the dressing and divide between four large plates. Place the chicken on top of the dressed salad leaves and serve straight away.

Serve with
Crusty French bread, sliced ciabatta or
wholemeal rolls

Tip

You can buy a bottle of French dressing, but it's quick and easy to make your own. Whisk together 5 ml/1 tsp of Dijon mustard, 15 ml/1 tbsp of white or red wine vinegar and a pinch of salt and pepper in a bowl. Gradually whisk in 90 ml/6 tbsp of light olive or sunflower oil. Alternatively, put all the ingredients in a screw-top jar and shake well. The dressing will keep in the fridge for up to a month.

lemon and herb chicken

Chicken and avocado wraps

Serves 4
Ready in 25 minutes

4 skinless, boneless chicken breasts

30 ml/2 tbsp soy sauce

30 ml/2 tbsp sunflower oil

1 red chilli, halved, seeded and finely chopped, or 5 ml/1 tsp chilli powder

Juice of 1 lime or 15 ml/1 tbsp bottled lemon juice

4 x 20 cm/8 in wheat tortillas

60 ml/4 tbsp Greek-style yoghurt or crème fraîche

1 head of radicchio or 1 Little Gem lettuce, sliced, or 100 g/4 oz bag of mixed salad leaves

2 ripe avocadoes, peeled and sliced

1 small red onion, peeled and thinly sliced

1 carrot, peeled and thinly sliced

Sprigs of coriander to garnish (optional)

1 Put the chicken breasts in a shallow non-metallic dish, large enough to hold them in a single layer.

2 Mix together the soy sauce, oil, chilli and lime or lemon juice. Spoon over the chicken and turn to coat thoroughly. Leave to marinate for at least 5 minutes or, if time allows, cover and chill in the fridge for up to 2 hours.

3 Heat a large non-stick frying pan or ridged cast iron grill pan. Remove the chicken from the marinade, add to the pan and cook over a moderately high heat for about 8 minutes on each side or until lightly browned and cooked through. Do not overcook or the chicken will be dry.

4 Remove the chicken from the pan and set aside. Wipe the pan clean with kitchen paper (paper towels).

5 Re-heat the pan and warm the tortillas, one at a time, for just a few seconds.

6 Spread the yoghurt or crème fraîche over one side of each tortilla, then fold into pockets. Cut the chicken into strips and use to fill the pockets with the salad leaves, avocado, red onion and carrot. Garnish with coriander sprigs, if liked. Serve straight away while the chicken is still warm.

Serve with

Guacamole or hummus to spoon on top

Tip

- Tortillas usually come in packs of eight. Re-seal the bag and pop the remaining four in the freezer for another time. Or, for those with larger appetites, divide the chicken mixture between all eight tortillas and serve them rolled up.

chicken and avocado wraps

Jazzy chicken pizzas

Serves 4
Ready in 15 minutes

2 x 23 cm/9 in margherita
pizzas, each about
325 g/11 oz

200 g/7 oz pack of ready-
cooked chicken strips

4 slices of ham, cut into
thick strips

150 g/5 oz pack of
Mozzarella cheese, sliced

8 cherry tomatoes

Freshly ground black pepper

1 Put two baking (cookie) sheets in the oven
on the top and middle shelves and preheat
to 220°C/425°F/gas 7/fan oven 200°C.

2 Unwrap the pizzas and arrange the chicken
and ham on top, followed by the Mozzarella
and tomatoes.

3 Place the pizzas on the hot oven sheets.
Bake for about 10 minutes or until the pizzas
have browned and the cheese is melted and
bubbling. Grind a little black pepper over and
serve straight away.

Serve with
**Watercress or a mixed salad and pots of
mayonnaise and pesto, if liked**

Tips

- Most supermarkets now stock
'basic' or 'economy' margherita
(cheese and tomato) pizzas at a
very reasonable price and it's
worth keeping a couple in the
freezer. Top these with your
favourite ingredients, such as
strips of ham and chopped
canned pineapple, spicy sliced
pepperami, or leftover
vegetables such as sliced
mushrooms and peppers.

- The baking sheets will catch any
drips from the pizzas and save
you cleaning the oven. If you
don't have any, the pizzas can be
cooked directly on the oven
shelves.

Jazzy chicken pizzas

Cajun chicken and veg

Serves 4
Ready in 30 minutes

15 ml/1 tbsp plain (all-purpose) flour

5 ml/1 tsp Cajun seasoning

Salt and freshly ground black pepper

450 g/1 lb mini chicken fillets, thawed if frozen

30 ml/2 tbsp oil

1 onion, peeled and finely chopped

225 g/8 oz/1 cup basmati rice, rinsed

450 ml/¾ pint/2 cups hot vegetable stock or water

400 g/14 oz/large can of red kidney beans, drained and rinsed

100 g/4 oz/⅔ cup frozen peas, thawed

100 g/4 oz/1 cup canned or thawed frozen sweetcorn

1 Preheat the oven to 200°C/400°F/gas 6/fan oven 180°C. Mix together the flour, Cajun seasoning and a pinch of salt. Trim the chicken fillets, if needed, then toss in the flour mixture.

2 Brush a non-stick baking tray with half the oil, then spread out the chicken fillets in a single layer. Bake in the oven for 18–20 minutes, turning them over half-way through the cooking time, until golden, crisp and cooked through (check this by cutting one in half).

3 Meanwhile, heat the remaining oil in a saucepan, add the onion and cook over a medium heat for 5 minutes, stirring frequently, until the onion is beginning to soften and colour.

4 Stir in the rice, then add the stock or water and a pinch of salt. Bring to the boil, then reduce the heat to low, cover the pan and cook for 10 minutes.

5 Stir in the beans, peas and sweetcorn, re-cover and cook for a further 4–5 minutes.

6 When the rice is ready, taste and adjust the seasoning if needed, then stir with a fork to fluff it up. Serve straight away.

Serve with
Tomato and red onion salad

Tip

- Cajun seasoning is a mixture of ground dried chillies, aromatic spices and herbs. You can buy it ready-made in small jars in the herb and spice section of the supermarket, or you can make your own by blending 2.5 ml/½ tsp chilli powder with a pinch each of paprika, cumin and dried mixed herbs.

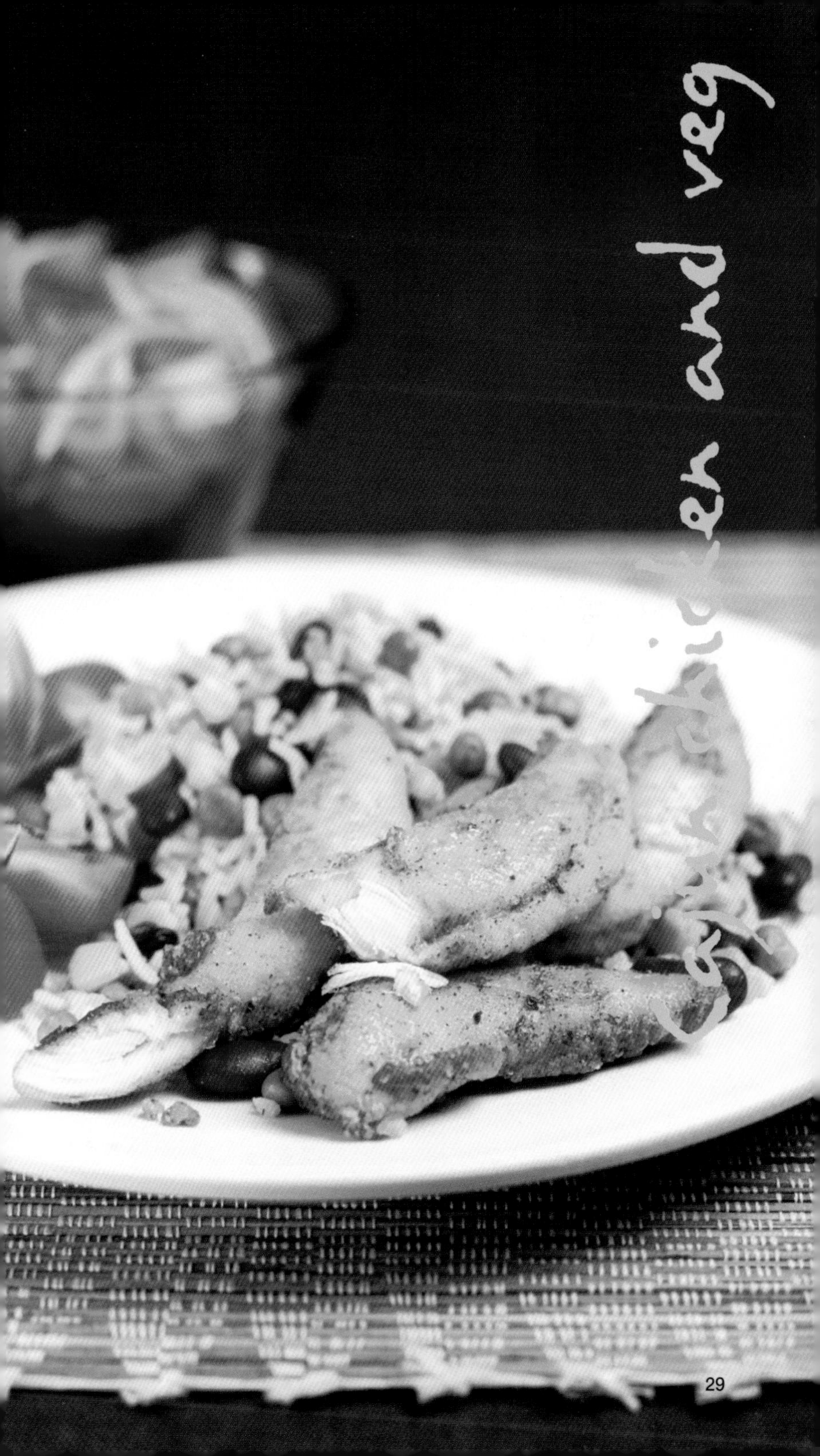
cajun chicken and veg

Oriental chicken noodles

Serves 4
Ready in 20 minutes

3 skinless, boneless chicken breasts or a 400g/14 oz pack of mini chicken fillets

15 ml/1 tbsp clear honey

45 ml/3 tbsp dark soy sauce

10 ml/2 tsp fresh or bottled lemon juice

10 ml/2 tsp fresh or bottled grated ginger or a large pinch of ground ginger

250 g/9 oz dried flat rice (cellophane) noodles or egg noodles

30 ml/2 tbsp oil

350 g/12 oz pack of mixed Chinese stir-fry vegetables

2.5 ml/½ tsp cornflour (cornstarch)

120 ml/4 fl oz/½ cup hot vegetable stock or water

1 Cut the chicken into strips about 1 cm/½ in wide. Mix together the honey, soy sauce, lemon juice and ginger in a bowl. Add the strips of chicken and toss to coat. Leave to marinate for a few minutes or, if time allows, cover and chill in the fridge for 2 hours.

2 Meanwhile, if using rice noodles, put them in a bowl and pour boiling water over. Soak for 3–4 minutes, then drain and rinse. If using egg noodles, cook them in a pan of boiling water for 3 minutes or according to the packet instructions. Drain thoroughly and set aside.

3 Heat half the oil in a large non-stick frying pan until hot. Remove the chicken from the bowl, reserving the marinade, and add to the pan. Stir-fry over a medium-high heat for 5 minutes or until the chicken is cooked through (keep turning and stirring the meat as it cooks). Remove from the pan with a slotted spoon and set aside on a plate.

4 Add the remaining oil to the pan, add the vegetables and stir-fry for 3–4 minutes over a medium-high heat. Turn the heat down a little, then return the chicken to the pan.

5 Blend the cornflour with the marinade mixture, then stir in the stock or water. Add this to the pan and bring to the boil, stirring. Add the noodles and stir for a minute or two until everything is cooked and piping hot. Serve straight away.

Tip

- Cellophane noodles are transparent flat noodles that usually only require soaking in boiling water to cook them. Check the packet instructions carefully as some need a slightly longer soaking time, so you may need to do this before starting to prepare the chicken.

Oriental chicken noodles

Caribbean chicken

Serves 4
Ready in 25 minutes

4 skinless, boneless chicken breasts or 16 chicken wings

Finely grated zest and juice of 1 lime

30 ml/2 tbsp clear honey

15 ml/1 tbsp fresh root ginger or bottled grated ginger

15 ml/1 tbsp pineapple juice (from the canned pineapple)

For the salsa

227 g/8 oz/small can of pineapple chunks in natural juice, drained and juice reserved

1 red chilli, halved, seeded and very finely chopped

15 ml/1 tbsp chopped fresh coriander (cilantro)

Salt and freshly ground black pepper

Wedges of lime, to garnish (optional)

1 Make two or three shallow slashes on each chicken breast or, if using chicken wings, trim off the tips, then make a slash through the skin of each. Put the chicken in a shallow non-metallic dish, large enough to hold them in a single layer.

2 Mix together half the lime zest, half the juice, the honey, ginger and pineapple juice in a bowl. Spoon over the chicken and turn to coat thoroughly. Leave to marinate for a few minutes while preparing the salsa.

3 To make the salsa, chop the pineapple chunks into smaller pieces and put in a bowl with the remaining lime zest and juice, the chilli and coriander. Lightly season with salt and pepper and mix well. Set aside for the flavours to mingle.

4 Preheat the grill (broiler) to medium-high and line the grill pan with foil. Remove the chicken from the marinade and arrange on the grill rack. Grill chicken breasts for 12–15 minutes until lightly browned and cooked through, turning once and basting, or chicken wings for 20 minutes, turning and basting with the marinade occasionally until well browned and crispy. Check that the juices run clear when the thickest part of the chicken is pierced with a small knife. Serve hot with the pineapple salsa, garnished with lime wedges, if liked.

Serve with
Boiled rice (see page 16) and freshly cooked green beans

Tip

- Buy single fresh chillies at the supermarket or from market-stall sellers for just a few pence (don't worry if your request for 'just one' raises eyebrows). Take great care when preparing chillies and always wash your hands well afterwards as the juices can cause burning irritation, especially if you touch your eyes or lips. If you enjoy spicy food, it's worthwhile investing in a jar of ready-chopped chillies; once opened, this will keep in the fridge for a couple of months. You'll need about half a teaspoonful for this recipe.

Caribbean chicken

Hot chicken salsa

Serves 2
Ready in 20 minutes

2 skinless, boneless chicken
breasts

30 ml/2 tbsp plain
(all-purpose) flour

15 ml/1 tbsp Cajun
seasoning

A pinch of salt

30 ml/2 tbsp oil

5 ml/1 tsp red or white wine
vinegar

1 garlic clove, peeled and
finely chopped, or 5 ml/1 tsp
garlic purée (optional)

4 ripe tomatoes, roughly
chopped

30 ml/2 tbsp chopped fresh
parsley

A large handful of baby
salad leaves

4 thick slices of rustic bread
such as ciabatta, lightly
toasted, if preferred

1 Cut each chicken breast in half lengthways
to give four roughly even-sized pieces.

2 Mix together the flour, Cajun seasoning and
salt, then use to coat the chicken.

3 Heat half the oil in a non-stick frying pan, add
the chicken and cook for 4–5 minutes on
each side until golden brown and cooked
through.

4 Meanwhile, using a fork, whisk together the
remaining oil, the vinegar and garlic, if using,
in a bowl. Add the tomatoes and parsley, then mix
together.

5 Divide the salad leaves between two of the
bread slices. Top each with two pieces of
chicken and spoon the tomato salsa over. Top
with the remaining bread slices and serve warm.

Tip

- You could also make this dish with
sliced turkey breast steaks or
escalopes. They are much thinner
than chicken breasts, so use
1½– 2 per person, cut each into three
strips and cook for just 2 minutes on
each side.

Hot chicken salsa

Thai green chicken curry

Serves 4
Ready in 25 minutes

25 ml/1 fl oz/1½ tbsp oil

450 g/1 lb chicken breast
fillets, trimmed if necessary

125 g/5 oz pack of baby
sweetcorn

45 ml/3 tbsp Thai green
curry paste

400 ml/14 oz/large can of
coconut milk

225 g/8 oz/small can of
sliced bamboo shoots,
drained

Shredded spring onions
(scallions), chilli dipping
sauce and wedges of lime,
to garnish (optional)

1 Heat 15 ml/1 tbsp of the oil in a non-stick frying pan, add the chicken and cook over a moderately high heat for 4–5 minutes, turning frequently, until lightly browned but not quite cooked through. Remove from the pan and set aside on a plate.

2 Add the remaining oil to the pan, add the sweetcorn and stir-fry over a moderate heat for 3 minutes. Add the curry paste and cook for a further 1 minute, stirring all the time.

3 Gradually stir in the coconut milk and bring to the boil. Stir in the chicken and bamboo shoots, lower the heat and simmer for 5–6 minutes or until the chicken and sweetcorn are cooked and tender. Serve hot, garnished with shredded spring onions, chilli dipping sauce and lime wedges, if liked.

Serve with
Boiled rice (see page 16) or noodles (see page 17)

Tips

- For a special occasion, garnish this dish with a sprinkling of chopped fresh coriander (cilantro) and some fine strips of spring onion (scallions). You could make the spring onion strips curly: drop them in icy water for about 5 minutes, then drain on kitchen paper (paper towels) before using. Some popadoms would also be good served with this.

- For vegetarians, substitute two 250 g/9 oz packs of smoked tofu with almonds and sesame seeds, cubed, for the chicken. Omit step 1 and stir-fry the tofu cubes with the sweetcorn.

Thai green chicken curry

Chicken and mushroom pie

> **Serves 4**
> **Ready in 1 hour**

375 g/13 oz pack of ready-rolled puff pastry (paste), chilled

25 g/1 oz/2 tbsp butter or 30 ml/2 tbsp oil

350 g/12 oz skinned and boned chicken thighs or 2 large skinless, boneless chicken breasts, cut into bite-sized pieces

2 medium leeks, washed and thinly sliced

225 g/8 oz button mushrooms, thickly sliced

1 garlic clove, peeled and crushed or finely chopped, or 5 ml/1 tsp garlic purée (paste)

200 g/7 oz/scant 1 cup cream cheese

2.5 ml/½ tsp dried mixed herbs

Salt and freshly ground black pepper

Beaten egg or milk, to glaze

Tip

- When preparing leeks, trim the root end and coarse tops and discard any tough outer leaves. The easiest way to clean them is to slit about halfway down the stalks lengthways, then to rinse well under cold running water.

1 Take the puff pastry out of the fridge and leave it at room temperature while preparing the filling (this will make it easy to unroll without cracking).

2 Heat half the butter or oil in a large non-stick frying pan. Add the chicken pieces and cook, stirring, over a medium heat for 2–3 minutes. Remove from the pan and set aside on a plate.

3 Heat the remaining butter or oil in the pan, add the leeks and mushrooms and cook for 5 minutes, stirring often, until soft. Stir in the garlic, then turn off the heat.

4 Add the cream cheese to the pan, letting it melt into the juices in the residual heat. Then stir in the herbs and salt and pepper to taste. Let the mixture cool for 10 minutes, then spoon into a large oval pie dish. Preheat the oven to 200°C/400°F/gas 6/fan oven 180°C.

5 Unroll the pastry and trim it to an oval about 5 cm/2 cm larger than the pie dish. Cut off a 2.5 cm/1 in strip from all round the oval. Dampen the edge of the dish with cold water using either a pastry brush or a piece of kitchen paper (paper towel) and press the strip of pastry on to the rim. Brush the pastry strip with beaten egg or milk, then position the pastry oval on top to make a lid. Press the edges together to seal and cut off any excess pastry with a sharp knife. Make a pattern around the rim with a fork. Brush the top with beaten egg or milk (if you don't have a pastry brush, leave out this step).

6 Stand the pie on a baking (cookie) sheet to catch any drips and make a slit in the middle to let steam escape and to prevent the pastry becoming soggy. Bake for 30–35 minutes or until the pastry is well risen and golden brown. Leave to stand for 5 minutes before cutting.

Serve with
Steamed mixed vegetables

chicken and mushroom pie

Herby turkey and bacon

Serves 2
Ready in 20 minutes

4 rashers (slices) of streaky
bacon, rinded

250 g/9 oz pack of fresh
filled tortellini

2 Little Gem lettuces or
1 Romaine lettuce, leaves
separated and torn into
smaller pieces

250 g/9 oz cooked turkey,
cut into bite-sized pieces

30 ml/2 tbsp herby Caesar
or your favourite salad
dressing

Freshly ground black pepper

1 Grill or fry the bacon until well browned and crisp. Leave to cool, then tear into pieces.

2 Meanwhile, simmer the tortellini in a large pan of boiling water for 3 minutes or according to the packet instructions until tender. Drain and rinse in cold water, then drain again.

3 Arrange the lettuce leaves in individual bowls.

4 Toss the turkey pieces in half the salad dressing, then add the bacon and tortellini and mix together. Spoon on top of the lettuce, then drizzle with the remaining dressing and season with pepper. Serve straight away.

Serve with
French bread

Tips

- Fresh pasta cooks in just a few minutes, so it's a great fix when you're in a hurry. If you don't have the time (or the inclination) to make a sauce or salad to serve with it, toss in a spoonful of French dressing and serve sprinkled with grated cheese.

- You probably won't need to season this dish with salt as the bacon will have plenty in it already.

- Two cooked skinless, boneless chicken breasts or 250 g/9 oz of leftover cooked chicken, cut into bite-sized pieces, may be used instead of the turkey.

Herby turkey and bacon

Sesame turkey stir-fry

Serves 4
Ready in 30 minutes

30 ml/2 tbsp sesame seeds

250 g/9 oz pack of fine or medium dried egg noodles

25 ml/1 fl oz/1½ tbsp oil

350 g/12 oz turkey escalopes, cut into thin strips

1 small red onion, peeled, halved and thinly sliced

2 large carrots, peeled and cut into matchstick-sized pieces

200 g/7 oz pack of mangetout (snow peas)

200 g/7 oz pack of baby sweetcorn, each cut into 4 pieces

1 fresh red chilli, halved, seeded and sliced, or 5 ml/1 tsp chilli powder

30 ml/2 tbsp clear honey

30 ml/ 2 tbsp fresh or bottled lemon juice

30 ml/2 tbsp soy sauce, plus extra for serving

30 ml/2 tbsp water

1 Dry-toast the sesame seeds in a large non-stick frying pan over a medium heat until golden, stirring all the time. Tip into a bowl and set aside.

2 Put the noodles in a pan and pour over plenty of boiling water. Bring back to the boil, then half-cover the pan with a lid and simmer for 2 minutes. Turn off the heat and leave the noodles for a further 3–4 minutes until cooked.

3 Meanwhile, heat half the oil in the frying pan, add the turkey and stir-fry over a medium-high heat for 3–4 minutes until golden brown. Lift out of the pan with a slotted spoon, leaving any juices behind, and set aside on a plate.

4 Add the remaining oil to the pan. Heat for a few seconds, then add the onion and stir-fry for 1 minute. Add the carrots and stir-fry for 1 more minute, then add the mangetout, sweetcorn and chilli. Cook for 2 more minutes, stirring often.

5 Mix together half the sesame seeds, the honey, lemon juice, soy sauce and water. Add this to the pan with the turkey and cook for 2–3 minutes or until everything is cooked through and hot.

6 Drain the noodles and divide between warmed plates or bowls. Top with the stir-fried turkey and vegetables, then scatter with the remaining toasted sesame seeds and serve with a small dish of soy sauce, if liked.

Tips

- Stir-frying is one of the fastest and healthiest methods of cooking, as you need only a little oil. Prepare all the ingredients before you start to cook: once stir-frying starts, there's no time for chopping and slicing.

- When toasting sesame seeds, watch them carefully as they can burn easily. Some supermarkets sell ready-toasted sesame seeds.

sesame turkey stir-fry

Meat

Make expensive meat go further by adding lots of starchy carbohydrates such as potatoes, pasta and rice and by serving it with plenty of vegetables. Do use the right cut of meat for your chosen recipes. For quick-cook dishes such as stir-fries, you need lean, tender cuts – these may seem pricey, but a little will go a long way. For stews and casseroles, choose cheaper cuts as they will be tenderised by long, slow cooking. Store meat in the coldest part of the fridge and, if raw, keep it away from cooked foods. Be guided by the 'use-by' date, but most joints, chops and steaks will keep in the fridge for 2–3 days.

Beef and potato curry

Serves 4
Ready in 45 minutes

15 ml/1 tbsp oil

1 large onion, peeled and finely chopped

2 garlic cloves, peeled and crushed or finely chopped

30–45 ml/2–3 tbsp medium curry powder

500 g/18 oz lean minced (ground) beef

2 potatoes, about 350 g/ 12 oz total weight, peeled and cut into 2 cm/¾ in cubes

225 g/8 oz/small can of chopped tomatoes

300 ml/½ pint/1¼ cups beef or vegetable stock or water

Salt and freshly ground black pepper

30 ml/2 tbsp chopped fresh coriander (cilantro), to garnish (optional)

1 Heat the oil in a large saucepan or non-stick frying pan, add the onion and cook over a medium heat for 5 minutes, stirring often, until softened.

2 Stir in the garlic and curry powder, then add the beef. Turn up the heat a little and cook for 5–6 minutes, stirring all the time and breaking up the meat with a wooden spoon, until browned and all the grains have separated.

3 Add the potatoes, tomatoes and stock or water and bring to the boil. Lower the heat until the mixture is bubbling gently, then half-cover the pan with a lid and cook for 20–25 minutes until the potatoes are tender.

4 Season to taste with salt and pepper and serve straight away, garnished with a scattering of fresh chopped coriander, if liked.

Serve with
Warm naan bread

Tip

- There are lots of curry powders and pastes available – some mild and subtle, others hot and spicy. Be on the safe side when using for the first time and add less rather than more!

beef and potato curry

Beef and mushroom noodles

Serves 4
Ready in 20 minutes

225 g/8 oz rump steak, trimmed

10 ml/2 tsp cornflour (cornstarch)

Salt and freshly ground black pepper

30 ml/2 tbsp oil

150 g/5 oz broccoli, cut into florets

75 ml/5 tbsp beef stock or water

150 g/5 oz mushrooms, sliced

1 bunch of spring onions (scallions), trimmed and sliced

15 ml/1 tbsp oyster sauce

3 x 150 g/5 oz packs of straight-to-wok medium or thick noodles

1 Slice the beef across the grain, then cut the slices into long, fine strips.

2 Mix together the cornflour and a little salt and pepper and toss the beef in this mixture until lightly coated.

3 Heat half the oil in a large non-stick frying pan over a medium-high heat. Add the beef and stir for about 2 minutes until browned. Remove from the pan and set aside on a plate.

4 Add the remaining oil to the pan with the broccoli and stock or water. Cover with a lid and cook for 3 minutes, lifting the lid and stirring a few times. Remove the lid, add the mushrooms and spring onions and stir-fry for 2 minutes.

5 Stir in the oyster sauce and the noodles, then return the beef to the pan. Cook for 2 more minutes until everything is hot and cooked through. Serve straight away on warmed plates.

Tips

- Tender, thin meat that can be cooked quickly over a high heat is best for stir-fries. These tend to be the more expensive cuts, but a little will stretch a long way. Instead of rump steak, you could use slightly cheaper 'minute' steak. This is thinly sliced beef that has been gently beaten with a meat mallet to tenderise it.

- Pork fillet or chicken breast can also be used in this dish. Or you could use cold roast beef, cut into strips, instead of steak and add it at the same time as the oyster sauce.

- A jar of oyster sauce will last for ages in the fridge and is great for loads of stir-fries and Chinese-style meals.

- Instead of straight-to-wok noodles, you could use a 250 g/9 oz pack of thick egg noodles. Cook in boiling stock or water for 3–4 minutes, then drain well, add to the pan and toss everything together before serving.

Beef and mushroom noodles

Beef goulash

15 ml/1 tbsp plain
(all-purpose) flour

Salt and freshly ground
black pepper

700 g/1½ lb stewing steak,
trimmed and cut into chunks

30 ml/2 tbsp oil

1 large onion, very thinly
sliced

1 garlic clove, peeled and
finely chopped or crushed,
or 5 ml/1 tsp garlic purée
(paste)

15 ml/1 tbsp ground paprika

5 ml/1 tsp dried mixed herbs

400 g/14 oz/large can of
chopped tomatoes

150 ml/¼ pint/⅔ cup beef
stock or water

1 large red or green (bell)
pepper (or 2 small peppers
of any colour), halved,
seeded and sliced

60 ml/4 tbsp soured (dairy
sour) cream or Greek-style
yoghurt (optional)

1 Preheat the oven to 160°C/325°F/gas 3/fan oven 145°C. Mix together the flour and a little salt and pepper and toss the beef in this mixture until lightly coated.

2 Heat half the oil in a deep ovenproof casserole dish (Dutch oven). Add the onion and cook gently for 7–8 minutes until it starts to soften and turn golden. Add the garlic and cook for 1 minute. Remove from the pan and set aside on a plate.

3 Heat the remaining oil in the casserole, then fry the beef over a high heat in two batches, turning often until browned on all sides. Stir in the paprika and herbs, then return the onion and garlic to the casserole. Stir in the tomatoes and stock or water and bring to the boil. Cover and cook in the oven for 1 hour.

4 Stir the sliced peppers into the casserole and return to the oven for 45 minutes or until both the meat and peppers are tender. Taste and re-season, if necessary, then stir in half the soured cream or yoghurt, if using. Spoon the rest on top and sprinkle with a pinch of paprika, if liked.

Serve with
Thick flat noodles (see page 17), jacket potatoes (see page 17), oven-baked rice (see page 66) or boiled rice (see page 16)

Tips

- You can buy stewing steak in thick slices or ready cubed. It may also be labelled as 'braising', 'casserole' or 'chuck' steak. You need to allow plenty of time for this dish, as it's the long, slow cooking that makes the meat tender.

- If you don't have a casserole dish or the use of an oven, simmer the goulash in a pan on the hob on the lowest possible heat – it should barely bubble. Keep the lid on and check and stir it a few times towards the end of the cooking time.

Beef goulash

Steak baguettes with onions

Serves 2
Ready in 15 minutes

1 onion, peeled, halved and thinly sliced

15 ml/1 tbsp self-raising flour

60 ml/4 tbsp oil

2 small baguettes or a short French stick, halved and split

60 ml/4 tbsp mayonnaise

2 handfuls of baby lettuce leaves

2 beef 'sandwich' steaks, each about 50 g/2 oz

Salt and freshly ground black pepper

1 Toss the onion slices in the flour to coat lightly. Heat the oil in a large non-stick frying pan until hot (check this by dropping in one of the onion slices – it should sizzle). Add half the onion slices, then turn down the heat a little and fry for 2–3 minutes, turning occasionally, until browned and crisp. Lift out with a slotted spoon, leaving most of the oil behind, then drain on kitchen paper (paper towels). Repeat with the remaining onions. Turn off the hob.

2 Toast the split baguettes for 1–2 minutes under a medium-hot grill (broiler) until golden. Leave to cool for a couple of minutes, then spread one side with the mayonnaise and top with lettuce.

3 Drain most of the oil from the frying pan, leaving no more than 15 ml/1 tbsp behind. Fry the steaks over a medium heat for 1–1½ minutes on each side. Place in the baguettes, season with salt and pepper, then spoon the crispy onions on top. Serve hot.

Serve with
Chips (fries)

Tips

- Really good chips are not easy to make, so it's best to buy some oven chips and follow the instructions on the packet.

- Take care when frying with oil and never leave it unattended. Turn off the hob if you need to do something else such as answer the phone.

- Tossing the onion slices in self-raising flour, then quickly frying them in hot oil makes them crisp and light. If you don't have any flour, fry the onions slowly over a low heat for about 10 minutes in 15 ml/1 tbsp of oil, stirring them often, until soft and golden.

Steak baguettes with onions

Chilli beef tortillas

Serves 2
Ready in 30 minutes

45 ml/3 tbsp oil

2 beef 'sandwich' steaks, each about 50 g/2 oz, trimmed and cut into 2.5 cm/1 in wide slices

1 red onion, peeled, halved and finely sliced

1 red (bell) pepper, halved, seeded and sliced

2 red chillies, halved, seeded and finely chopped, or 5 ml/1 tsp chilli powder

5 ml/1 tsp paprika

2.5 ml/½ tsp ground cumin

Salt and freshly ground black pepper

4 x 20 cm/8 in wheat tortillas

1 ripe avocado, halved, peeled and sliced

Grated Cheddar cheese

Shredded spring onions (scallions) and fresh coriander (cilantro) leaves, to garnish (optional)

1 Heat 15 ml/1 tbsp of the oil in a non-stick frying pan. Add the beef and cook over a medium-high heat for 2–3 minutes until browned. Remove from the pan and set aside on a plate. Turn down the heat a little.

2 Add the remaining oil to the pan. Add the onion and cook for 3 minutes, stirring often. Add the red pepper and fresh chillies, if using, and cook for a further 3–4 minutes, until almost tender. Stir in the chilli powder, if using, and the other spices and some seasoning. Return the beef to the pan and cook over a low heat for about 1 minute until everything is really hot.

3 Meanwhile, heat the tortillas one at a time in a dry frying pan for 30 seconds on each side. Spoon the beef mixture into the centre of each one, then add some avocado slices, some Cheddar and spring onions and coriander, if using. Roll up and eat straight away.

Tips

- It's difficult to cook the beef mixture and heat the tortillas at the same time, so get someone to help you if you can. If you have only one frying pan, tip the beef mixture into a hot bowl (rinse it out with near-boiling water first) and cover with a plate or lid to keep it as hot as possible. Wipe the pan clean with kitchen paper (paper towels), then heat the tortillas.

- Paprika and cumin add a subtle spicy flavour but, if you don't have them, simply leave them out. The tortillas will still taste good!

chilli beef tortillas

Thai beef salad

Serves 4
Ready in 20 minutes

4 x 125 g/4½ oz beef
medallion steaks

10 ml/2 tsp oil

Salt and freshly ground
black pepper

150 g/5 oz bag of
beansprouts, rinsed

100 g/4 oz bag of herb salad
or baby salad leaves

100 g/4 oz red grapes,
halved

60 ml/4 tbsp salad dressing

1 Rub the steaks on both sides with the oil, then season with salt and pepper.

2 Heat a large non-stick frying pan for a few minutes over a high heat, add the steaks, then turn down the heat to medium. Cook for 3–4 minutes on each side for a medium steak. Lift out of the pan and on to a chopping board. Leave to 'rest' for 5 minutes (this helps tenderise the meat), then slice thinly.

3 Meanwhile, mix together the beansprouts, salad leaves, grapes and dressing. Divide between four plates and top with the sliced beef. Serve straight away.

Tips

- Cooking steak to perfection is tricky and one of the easiest ways to check it's done to your liking is to cut into it and have a look. Much depends on the thickness of the steak. As a rough guide, a 2 cm/¾ in thick steak takes about 2 minutes (frying or grilling) on each side for rare, 3–4 minutes for medium and 5–6 minutes for well done.

- Choose a spicy Thai-style salad dressing for this dish, or make a simple one yourself by whisking together 45 ml/3 tbsp of light olive or sunflower oil, 15 ml/1 tbsp of lime juice or 10 ml/2 tsp of red or white wine vinegar, 5 ml/1 tsp of grated fresh root ginger or bottled ginger or a pinch of ground ginger, a tiny pinch of curry powder, salt and freshly ground black pepper.

thai beef salad

Italian baked meatballs

Serves 4
Ready in 45 minutes

350 g/12 oz lean minced (ground) beef

1 garlic clove, peeled and crushed or finely chopped

5 ml/1 tsp dried mixed herbs

Salt and freshly ground black pepper

10 ml/2 tsp oil

250 g/9 oz dried pasta shapes

400 g/14 oz/large can of chopped tomatoes

100 g/4 oz Mozzarella or Cheddar cheese, thinly sliced

15 ml/1 tbsp chopped fresh herbs such as parsley or thyme, to garnish (optional)

1 Put the beef, garlic and herbs in a bowl. Season with salt and pepper, then mix together using your hands. Shape into about 20 balls and place on a plate.

2 Preheat the oven to 190°C/375°F/gas 5/fan oven 170°C. Heat the oil in a large non-stick frying pan, add the meatballs and cook for 7–8 minutes, turning frequently, until browned all over. Remove from the pan and drain on kitchen paper (paper towels).

3 Meanwhile, cook the pasta in a large pan of boiling water for 7 minutes or until almost tender. Drain thoroughly, then return to the pan. Add the meatballs and chopped tomatoes and mix gently together, taking care not to break up the meatballs.

4 Tip the mixture into an ovenproof dish and spread out evenly. Arrange the cheese slices on top and bake for around 20 minutes until golden brown and bubbling. Garnish with fresh herbs, if liked.

Serve with
Garlic bread and salad

 ## Tips

- For a really quick version of this dish, use a 350 g/12 oz pack of Swedish meatballs and a 250 g/9 oz pack of fresh ravioli and simply mix with the chopped tomatoes before putting in the baking dish.

- It's easy to make your own garlic bread. Mix 75 g/3 oz of butter or sunflower margarine with 2 crushed or chopped garlic cloves or 10 ml/2 tsp of garlic purée (paste), salt and freshly ground black pepper. Using a sharp knife, make cuts along a French stick about 2.5 cm/1 in apart, as if you were slicing it but not right through (the loaf should stay joined at the base). Spread each slice with garlic butter on both sides. Wrap in foil (make sure first that the loaf will fit in the oven – if not, cut it into two smaller lengths) and cook in the oven below the meatballs for about 15 minutes.

Italian baked meatballs

Lamb kofte kebabs

**Serves 4
Ready in 30 minutes**

500 g/1 lb 2 oz pack of minced (ground) lamb

1 garlic clove, peeled and finely chopped or crushed, or 5 ml/1 tsp garlic purée (paste)

2.5 cm/1 in piece of fresh root ginger, grated, or 5 ml/1 tsp ginger purée (paste)

5 ml/1 tsp ground cumin (optional)

2.5 ml/½ tsp chilli powder

Salt and freshly ground pepper

15 ml/1 tbsp oil

4 pitta breads

150 ml/¼ pint/⅔ cup Greek-style yoghurt

30 ml/2 tbsp chopped fresh coriander (cilantro)

Shredded lettuce and thinly sliced red (bell) pepper or other favourite salad ingredients

Wedges of lemon, to garnish (optional)

1 Put the lamb, garlic, ginger, cumin, if using, and chilli powder in a bowl. Season with salt and pepper, then mix together using your hands. Shape into about 40 small balls and place on a plate.

2 Heat the oil in a large non-stick frying pan, add the meatballs and cook for 8–10 minutes, turning frequently, until browned all over and cooked through (check this by cutting a meatball in half; it should be brown throughout and not pink). Using a slotted spoon to let the fat drain away, lift the meatballs on to a plate lined with kitchen paper (paper towels).

3 Meanwhile, warm the pitta breads for a few seconds under the grill (broiler) or in the microwave (this isn't essential but it does make it easier to open them up). Cut each in half and open to make a pocket.

4 Mix together the yoghurt and coriander and season with a little salt and pepper. Fill each pitta pocket with some shredded salad and pepper slices, drizzle with the yoghurt mixture, then add five hot lamb meatballs to each. Serve straight away, garnished with lemon wedges, if liked.

Tips

- If you haven't any fresh coriander, stir a large spoonful of chutney or a teaspoonful of mint sauce into the yoghurt.

- There are lots of different types of pitta breads. Try sesame seed, herb or garlic-flavoured or wholemeal ones for a change.

lamb kofte kebabs

Baked lamb biryani

**Serves 4
Ready in 1¼ hours**

25 ml/1 fl oz/1½ tbsp oil

450 g/1 lb lean lamb, trimmed and cubed

1 large onion, sliced

2 carrots, peeled and thickly sliced

100 g/4 oz button mushrooms, halved

30 ml/2 tbsp mild curry paste

400 g/14 oz/large can of chopped tomatoes

300 ml/½ pint/1¼ cups hot vegetable stock

100 g/4 oz/⅔ cup frozen peas, thawed

Salt and freshly ground black pepper

225 g/8 oz/1 cup basmati rice, rinsed

600 ml/1 pint/2½ cups water

2.5 ml/½ tsp ground turmeric

15 ml/1 tbsp chopped fresh coriander (cilantro), to garnish (optional)

1 Heat 15 ml/1 tbsp of the oil in a frying pan, add the lamb and cook over a medium-high heat for 3–4 minutes, turning often, until browned all over. Lift out of the pan using a slotted spoon to leave behind any oil and juices and set aside on a plate.

2 Add the remaining oil to the pan. Add the onion and cook gently for 7–8 minutes until beginning to soften and turn golden.

3 Stir in the carrots, mushrooms and curry paste and cook for a further 1 minute.

4 Add the tomatoes and stock and bring to the boil. Cover the pan and simmer gently for 30 minutes, then turn off the heat, stir in the peas and season with salt and pepper to taste.

5 While the lamb is cooking, put the rice, water and turmeric in a saucepan. Bring to the boil, then cover and simmer very gently for 7 minutes or until the rice is almost tender. Drain off the excess water.

6 Preheat the oven to 160°C/325°F/gas 3/fan oven 145°C. Spoon half of the rice into a lightly greased casserole dish (Dutch oven). Carefully pour the lamb curry on top, then cover with the rest of the rice. Cover and bake for 30 minutes, checking after 20 minutes and adding a little more stock or water if needed (there should be just enough liquid for the rice to finish cooking).

7 When the biryani is ready, stir it well and garnish with coriander, if liked.

Tips

- The curry mixture can be made in advance, cooled and kept covered in the fridge for up to 24 hours ahead, then the dish finished later by layering with the rice and baking.

- This dish is also good made with cheaper cuts of meat such as boneless turkey thigh meat, or you could make a vegetarian version with one 400 g/14 oz/ can each of chickpeas and black-eyed beans or red kidney beans, drained and rinsed. Add these with the carrots and mushrooms and simmer the curry mixture for just 20 minutes.

Baked lamb beryani

Hoisin lamb kebabs

Serves 4
Ready in 30 minutes

550 g/1¼ lb thickly cut lamb
steaks or shoulder of lamb

75 ml/5 tbsp hoisin sauce

1 bunch spring onions
(scallions), trimmed

Shreds of fresh red chilli and
spring onions, to garnish
(optional)

1 Trim the lamb of any excess fat, then cut into bite-sized pieces. Put the meat in a bowl with the hoisin sauce, then stir to ensure it is well coated. Leave to marinate at room temperature for about 15 minutes or, if time, in the fridge for up to 4 hours (this will help to tenderise and flavour the meat).

2 Meanwhile, if you are using wooden skewers, soak eight in cold water (this helps to stop them charring when grilling). Cut each spring onion widthways into 3 pieces.

3 When ready to cook, preheat the grill (broiler) to a high setting. Remove the lamb from the marinade and thread on to the wooden skewers or on four long flat metal skewers, alternating with the spring onions. Grill for 10–12 minutes, turning often and basting with the marinade, until browned and cooked through.

4 Serve straight away, garnished with shredded red chilli and spring onions, if liked.

Serve with
Boiled rice (see page 16) sprinkled with
sesame seeds

 Tips

- Hoisin sauce is a thick and sticky brownish-red sauce, usually made from soy beans, garlic, chilli, sugar and vinegar. You'll find it among the Chinese cooking sauces at the supermarket. Once opened, keep it in the fridge – it will last for several months.

- For spicy yoghurt-crusted kebabs, use 75 ml/5 tbsp of Greek-style yoghurt mixed with 15 ml/1 tbsp of fresh or bottled lemon juice and 10 ml/2 tsp of curry paste instead of the hoisin sauce.

- This dish is also good made with lean pork such as tenderloin.

hoisin lamb kebabs

Moroccan spiced lamb

Serves 4
Ready in 20 minutes

Finely grated zest and juice
of 1 lemon

1 small fresh red chilli,
halved, seeded and finely
chopped, or 2.5 ml/½ tsp
chilli powder

2.5 ml/½ tsp ground
cinnamon

4 boneless lamb steaks

Salt and freshly ground
black pepper

15 ml/1 tbsp oil

60 ml/4 tbsp water

Sprigs of fresh coriander
(cilantro), to garnish
(optional)

For the couscous

400 ml/14 fl oz/1¾ cups hot
vegetable stock or water

10 ml/2 tsp oil

A pinch of dried mixed herbs

A pinch of ground turmeric

250 g/9 oz/1½ cups
couscous

1 Mix together the lemon zest, chilli and cinnamon. Press the mixture into both sides of the lamb steaks, then season with a little salt and pepper. Leave the flavours to mingle for a few minutes.

2 Meanwhile, begin cooking the couscous. Pour the stock or water into a saucepan (add a pinch of salt if using water). Add 10 ml/2 tsp oil, the dried herbs and turmeric, then bring to the boil. Pour in the couscous in a steady stream and stir well. Turn off the heat, cover with a lid and leave to stand for 5 minutes.

3 Heat 15 ml/1 tbsp oil in a large non-stick frying pan, add the steaks and fry for 4–5 minutes on each side, depending on their thickness and how well you like your meat cooked. Add half the lemon juice and the water to the pan and bubble for 1 minute.

4 Sprinkle the remaining lemon juice over the couscous, then heat gently for 1 minute, stirring and separating the grains with a fork.

5 Divide the couscous between four plates, top with the lamb, cut into thick chunks and spoon the cooking juices over the meat. Garnish with coriander, if liked.

Serve with
A sliced tomato and red onion salad

Tips

- Try adding some thawed frozen peas to the boiling stock when stirring in the couscous.

Moroccan spiced lamb

Sweet and sour lamb chops

Serves 4
Ready in 45 minutes

175 g/6 oz/¾ cup long-grain rice

450 ml/¾ pint/2 cups vegetable stock

Salt and freshly ground black pepper

4 carrots, peeled and quartered

15 ml/1 tbsp oil

8 lamb chops or cutlets

15 ml/1 tbsp balsamic vinegar

15 ml/1 tbsp caster (superfine) sugar

1 Preheat the oven to 190°C/375°F/gas 5/fan oven 170°C. Put the rice in a large ovenproof casserole dish (Dutch oven) with a capacity of about 2.25 litres/4 pints/10 cups. Stir in the stock and a little salt and pepper. Cover with a lid or foil and put on the shelf just below the middle of the oven.

2 Toss the carrots in 10 ml/2 tsp of the oil, then place them in a large roasting tin. Season generously with salt and pepper. When the rice has been cooking for 15 minutes, put the carrots on the top shelf of the oven. Cook for 15 minutes, turning them half-way through the cooking time.

3 Heat the remaining oil in a large non-stick frying pan over a medium-high heat. Add the lamb and cook for about 1 minute on each side or until they are lightly browned and the fat is crisp.

4 Push the carrots to one side of the roasting tin, then add the chops in a single layer. Drizzle the vinegar over the chops, then sprinkle with the sugar. Cook for a further 10 minutes or until the meat and carrots are browned and cooked through and the rice is tender.

5 Fluff up the rice with a fork before serving with the chops and carrots.

Tips

- If you prefer your lamb medium-rare, cook for 7–8 minutes in the oven; for well-done meat, cook for 12 minutes.

- To add more flavour to the rice, heat 15 ml/1 tbsp of oil in a large non-stick frying pan and gently cook 1 small onion, peeled and finely chopped, over a medium heat for 7–8 minutes or until just beginning to brown. Stir in the rice and cook for a few more seconds. Transfer to the casserole dish and stir in the stock.

sweet and sour lamb chops

Spicy lamb skewers

Serves 4
Ready in 20 minutes

550 g/1¼ lb thickly cut lamb
steaks or lean boneless leg
or shoulder of lamb

2 garlic cloves, peeled and
crushed or finely chopped,
or 10 ml/2 tsp garlic purée
(paste)

5 ml/1 tsp dried mixed herbs

5 ml/1 tsp ground cumin

5 ml/1 tsp ground paprika,
plus extra for sprinkling

2.5 ml/½ tsp ground turmeric

15 ml/1 tbsp oil

15 ml/1 tbsp fresh or bottled
lemon juice

Salt and freshly ground
black pepper

Bay leaves, to garnish
(optional)

For the salad

15 ml/1 tbsp oil

5 ml/1 tsp balsamic or
wine vinegar

1 small red onion, peeled,
halved and thinly sliced

2 oranges, peeled and cut
into segments

1 pink grapefruit, peeled and
cut into segments

1 bag or bunch of
watercress

1 Trim the lamb of any excess fat and cut into large chunks. Place in a non-metallic bowl. Mix together the garlic, herbs, cumin, paprika, turmeric, oil and lemon juice. Drizzle over the meat, turning to make sure it is well coated. Cover and leave to marinate for at least 2 hours, or preferably overnight in the fridge.

2 Thread the lamb on to four metal skewers (or wooden ones soaked in cold water). Season lightly with salt and pepper.

3 Line a grill (broiler) pan with foil, then grill the skewers under a medium-high heat, turning frequently, for 6–7 minutes or until just cooked through.

4 Meanwhile, to make the salad, whisk together the oil and vinegar in a salad bowl. Add the onion and toss in the dressing, then add the remaining salad ingredients and toss to mix well.

5 Sprinkle the lamb skewers with a little extra paprika, if liked, and serve them hot, garnished with bay leaves, if liked, with the salad.

Tip

- Marinating allows the flavours to penetrate the meat and tenderises it at the same time, so don't miss out this step. If you are in a hurry, let the meat marinate at room temperature for 15 minutes. When marinating overnight in the fridge, cover the bowl tightly with clingfilm (plastic wrap) to stop the spicy smell being absorbed by other foods.

spicy lamb skewers

Moussaka-filled aubergines

Serves 4
Ready in 1½ hours

45 ml/3 tbsp oil

1 onion, peeled and finely chopped

350 g/12 oz minced (ground) lamb

2.5 ml/½ tsp ground cinnamon (optional)

300 ml/½ pint/1¼ cups lamb or vegetable stock

400 g/14 oz/large can of chopped tomatoes

30 ml/2 tbsp chopped fresh parsley or 5 ml/1 tsp dried mixed herbs

Salt and freshly ground black pepper

2 aubergines

40 g/1½ oz/3 tbsp butter or sunflower margarine

40 g/1½ oz/4 tbsp plain (all-purpose) flour

450 ml/¾ pint/2 cups milk

1 egg, lightly beaten

60 ml/4 tbsp grated Cheddar cheese

Sprigs of parsley, to garnish (optional)

1 Heat 15 ml/1 tbsp of the oil in a saucepan, add the onion and cook for 3–4 minutes over a medium heat. Add the mince and cook for a further 4–5 minutes, stirring all the time and breaking up the meat with a wooden spoon, until browned and all the grains have separated.

2 Stir in the cinnamon, then add the stock, tomatoes, herbs and seasoning to taste. Half-cover the pan with a lid and simmer for 30 minutes, stirring occasionally.

3 Meanwhile, cut the aubergines in half lengthways. Heat the remaining oil in a large non-stick frying pan, add the aubergines flesh-sides down and cook for about 5 minutes until golden. Turn over and cook the rounded sides for 3–4 minutes. Place the aubergines, cut-sides up, in an ovenproof dish. Preheat the oven to 200°C/400°F/gas 6/fan oven 180°C.

4 To make the white sauce, put the butter or margarine, flour and milk in a saucepan and cook over a medium heat, stirring all the time, until the sauce bubbles and thickens. Remove from the heat and leave for 2–3 minutes, stirring occasionally, then whisk in the egg and season with salt and pepper.

5 Spoon the meat sauce over the aubergines, then top with the white sauce. Sprinkle the Cheddar over the top. Place in the oven and cook for 20–25 minutes or until the topping is golden brown. Garnish with sprigs of fresh parsley, if liked, and serve.

Serve with
Boiled rice flavoured with a pinch of ground turmeric (see page 16) or Greek bread

Tips

- Use minced beef instead of lamb, if you prefer.

- Make double the quantity of the meat sauce and freeze half for another meal. It can be served simply with pasta and a sprinkling of grated cheese.

- Greek *daktyla* goes well with this dish. It is a sesame-coated bread usually made with a blend of white and wholemeal flour and ground cornmeal.

Moussaka-filled aubergines

Thai-style pork

Serves 4
Ready in 25 minutes

5 ml/1 tsp oil

450 g/1 lb minced (ground) pork

1 red (bell) pepper, halved, seeded and chopped

150 g/5 oz button mushrooms, wiped and sliced

15 ml/1 tbsp cornflour (cornstarch)

30 ml/2 tbsp soy sauce

Juice of 1 lime or 30 ml/ 2 tbsp fresh or bottled lemon juice

150 ml/¼ pint/⅔ cup vegetable stock or water

30 ml/2 tbsp chopped fresh coriander (cilantro) or parsley, plus a few sprigs to garnish

Salt and freshly ground black pepper

1 Heat the oil in a large non-stick frying pan. Add the pork and cook for 5–6 minutes, stirring all the time and breaking up the meat with a wooden spoon, until browned and all the grains have separated.

2 Add the red pepper and mushrooms and cook, stirring, for 2–3 minutes.

3 Blend the cornflour to a smooth paste with the soy sauce, then stir in the lime or lemon juice and stock or water. Pour into the pan and simmer for 10 minutes.

4 Stir in the coriander and parsley, then season to taste with salt and pepper. Serve straight away, garnished with a few herb sprigs.

Serve with
Boiled rice (see page 16) or noodles (see page 17)

Tips

- Always buy good-quality 'extra-lean' pork mince. It may cost a little more, but is better value as it contains less fat.

- Lamb or beef mince may be used instead of pork in this dish, if preferred.

Thai-style pork

Crispy pork and noodles

Serves 4
Ready in 20 minutes

1 egg white

A pinch of salt

15 ml/1 tbsp cornflour
(cornstarch)

350 g/12 oz pork fillet, cut
into thin strips

30 ml/2 tbsp oil

1 large carrot, peeled and
cut into thin matchsticks

150 g/5 oz pack of
mangetout (snow peas), cut
into thin strips

1 small red or yellow (bell)
pepper, halved, seeded and
cut into thin strips

4 spring onions (scallions),
trimmed and cut into
thin strips

15 ml/1 tbsp grated fresh
root ginger or bottled ginger

15 ml/1 tbsp soy sauce

Juice of 1 small orange or
75 ml/5 tbsp orange juice
from a carton

45 ml/3 tbsp vegetable
stock or water

1 Lightly whisk the egg white with the salt and 10 ml/2 tsp of the cornflour in a bowl with a fork. Add the pork and turn to coat evenly.

2 Heat the oil over a medium-high heat in a large non-stick frying pan until hot (the meat should sizzle when added to the pan). Add the pork and fry for 2–3 minutes until crispy. Lift out with a slotted spoon and drain on kitchen paper (paper towels).

3 Add a little more oil to the pan, if needed, so that there is about 15 ml/1 tbsp. Add the carrot, mangetout, pepper strips and spring onions and stir-fry for 2–3 minutes.

4 Blend the remaining cornflour with the ginger and soy sauce, then stir in the orange juice and stock or water. Add to the pan and stir until bubbling.

5 Stir in the pork and cook for a further minute or two or until everything is hot and cooked through. Serve straight away.

Serve with
Egg noodles

Tip

- A 250 g/9 oz pack of egg noodles will serve four people and take about 4 minutes to cook – start boiling them after frying the pork. They're made from wheat flour, eggs and a few seasonings so, if you are eating with someone who has a wheat or gluten allergy, choose rice noodles instead.

crispy pork and noodles

Ham pasta salad

**Serves 4
Ready in 20 minutes**

250 g/9 oz dried pasta
shapes such as shells or
quills

45 ml/3 tbsp salad dressing

175 g/6 oz ham, diced

1 yellow (bell) pepper,
halved, seeded and diced

20 cherry tomatoes, halved

2 Little Gem lettuces,
washed

30 ml/2 tbsp chopped or
torn fresh basil leaves
(optional)

1 Cook the pasta in a large pan of boiling water for 10 minutes, or according to the packet instructions, until al dente (tender but firm to the bite). Drain in a colander, then briefly and gently rinse under cold water and drain again thoroughly.

2 Tip into a large bowl and toss with the salad dressing to prevent sticking.

3 Add the ham, diced pepper and tomatoes. Tear one of the lettuces into large pieces and add to the bowl with the basil, if using. Toss together well.

4 Line four individual bowls with the leaves from the other lettuce, then divide the salad between them. Serve straight away.

Serve with
Crusty wholemeal rolls or French bread

Tip

- You can use a bought dressing for this salad, or a classic French dressing (see page 22). For an Italian-style dressing, whisk 30 ml/ 2 tbsp of olive oil with 10 ml/2 tsp of balsamic vinegar, a tiny pinch of dried oregano or mixed herbs and a crushed garlic clove or 5 ml/1 tsp of garlic purée (paste). Add a few chopped olives, if liked.

Ham pasta salad

Big breakfast baguette

Serves 4
Ready in 30 minutes

1 large baguette

8 chipolata sausages

4 rashers (slices) of back bacon, rinded

A large knob of butter or sunflower margarine, about 25 g/1 oz/2 tbsp

4 eggs, lightly beaten

30 ml/2 tbsp chopped fresh parsley (optional)

Salt and freshly ground black pepper

16 cherry tomatoes

1 Cut the baguette in half lengthways, then horizontally, so you have four pieces. Line the grill (broiler) pan with foil and preheat the grill to medium. Place the sausages and bacon on the rack and cook, turning regularly, until the sausages are golden brown and cooked through and the bacon is crispy. Remove from the grill and set aside (if you can, keep them warm in the oven at a low temperature).

2 Meanwhile, gently melt the butter or margarine in a pan, preferably non-stick. Pour in the eggs then, using a wooden spoon, stir almost constantly until the eggs are just beginning to set. Lift the pan off the heat and stir in the parsley, salt and pepper. Continue to stir for about 1 minute as the eggs will carry on cooking even when not on the heat.

3 Place the baguette slices, cut-sides up, on the grill to toast. Remove, then add the tomatoes to the grill pan and cook for a few minutes until they start to split (or you can put them on for about 1 minute, then turn off the heat and leave them to cook in the residual heat while assembling the baguettes).

4 Place the toasted baguette slices on four serving plates. Top each one with the scrambled eggs. Slice the sausages horizontally and place on top of the egg with the bacon. Serve straight away with the grilled tomatoes.

Tip

- Chipolatas are small British sausages about half the thickness of a normal pork sausage. You can, of course, use ordinary sausages, but they'll take a little longer to cook.

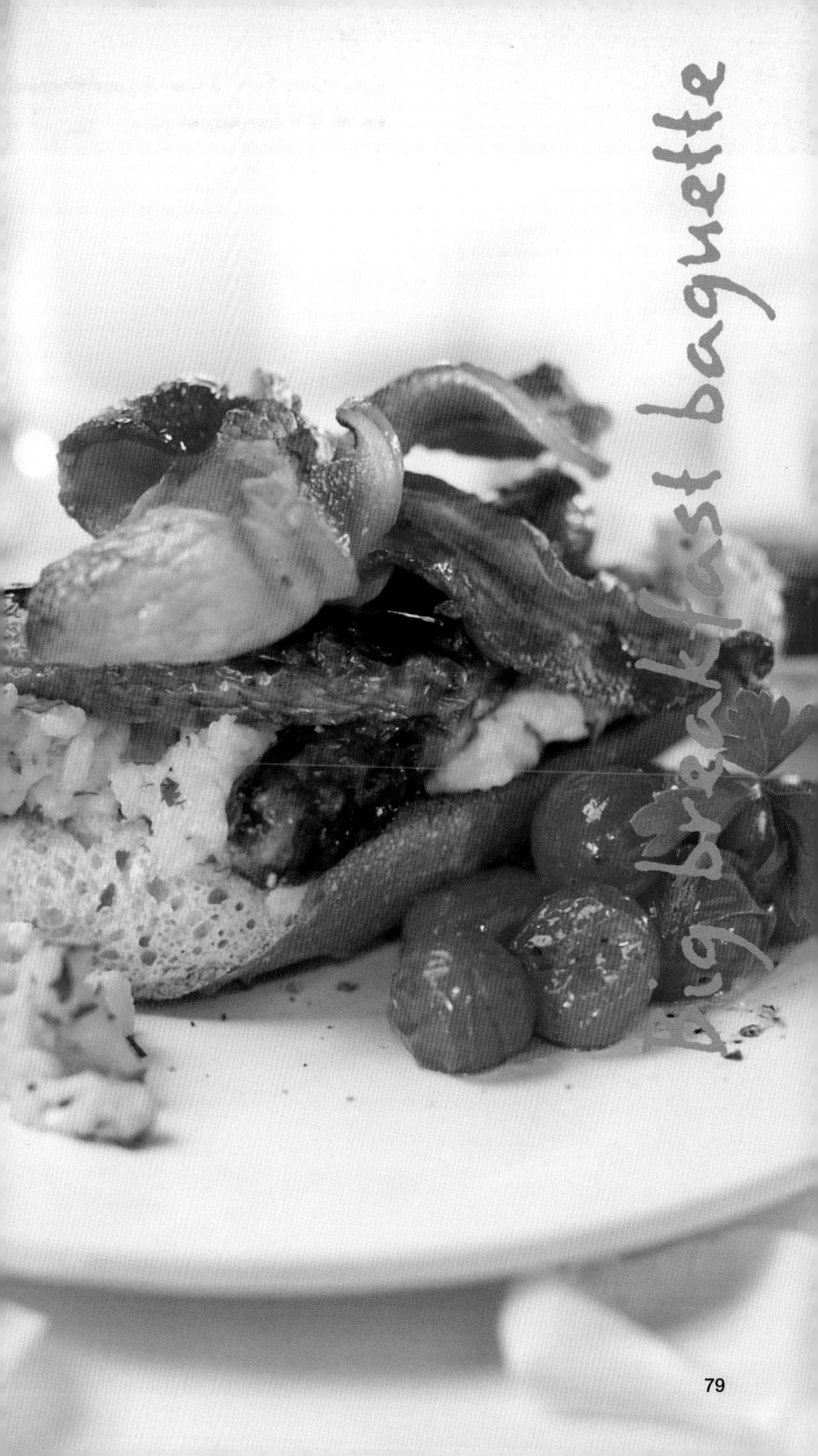

breakfast baguette

Spicy sausage pasta

**Serves 4
Ready in 40 minutes**

20 large dried pasta shells

450 g/1 lb spicy sausages

2.5 ml/½ tsp dried mixed herbs

50 g/2 oz/½ cup freshly grated Parmesan or mature Cheddar cheese

25 g/1 oz/2 tbsp butter or margarine

25 g/1 oz/¼ cup plain (all-purpose) flour

300 ml/½ pint/1¼ cups milk

Salt and freshly ground black pepper

1 Preheat the oven to 200°C/400°F/gas 6/fan oven 180°C.

2 Cook the pasta shells in a large pan of boiling water for 8 minutes, or according to the packet instructions, until al dente (tender but firm to the bite). Drain in a colander, then briefly and gently rinse under cold water and drain thoroughly.

3 Squeeze the meat out of the sausage skins into a bowl and mix with the herbs and half the cheese. Stuff the sausage mixture into the pasta shells and place in a lightly greased baking dish.

4 Put the butter, flour and milk in a pan, season generously and heat, stirring all the time, until the sauce bubbles and thickens. Drizzle the sauce over the filled shells, then sprinkle the remaining cheese over.

5 Bake in the oven for 20 minutes or until golden brown. Serve hot.

**Serve with
A mixed salad**

Tips

- You'll need very large pasta shells, about 4 cm/1½ in long; don't try stuffing smaller shells – it would be much too fiddly.

- Choose good-quality sausages for this recipe; economy ones contain a higher proportion of fat and cheap fillers, which would spoil this dish.

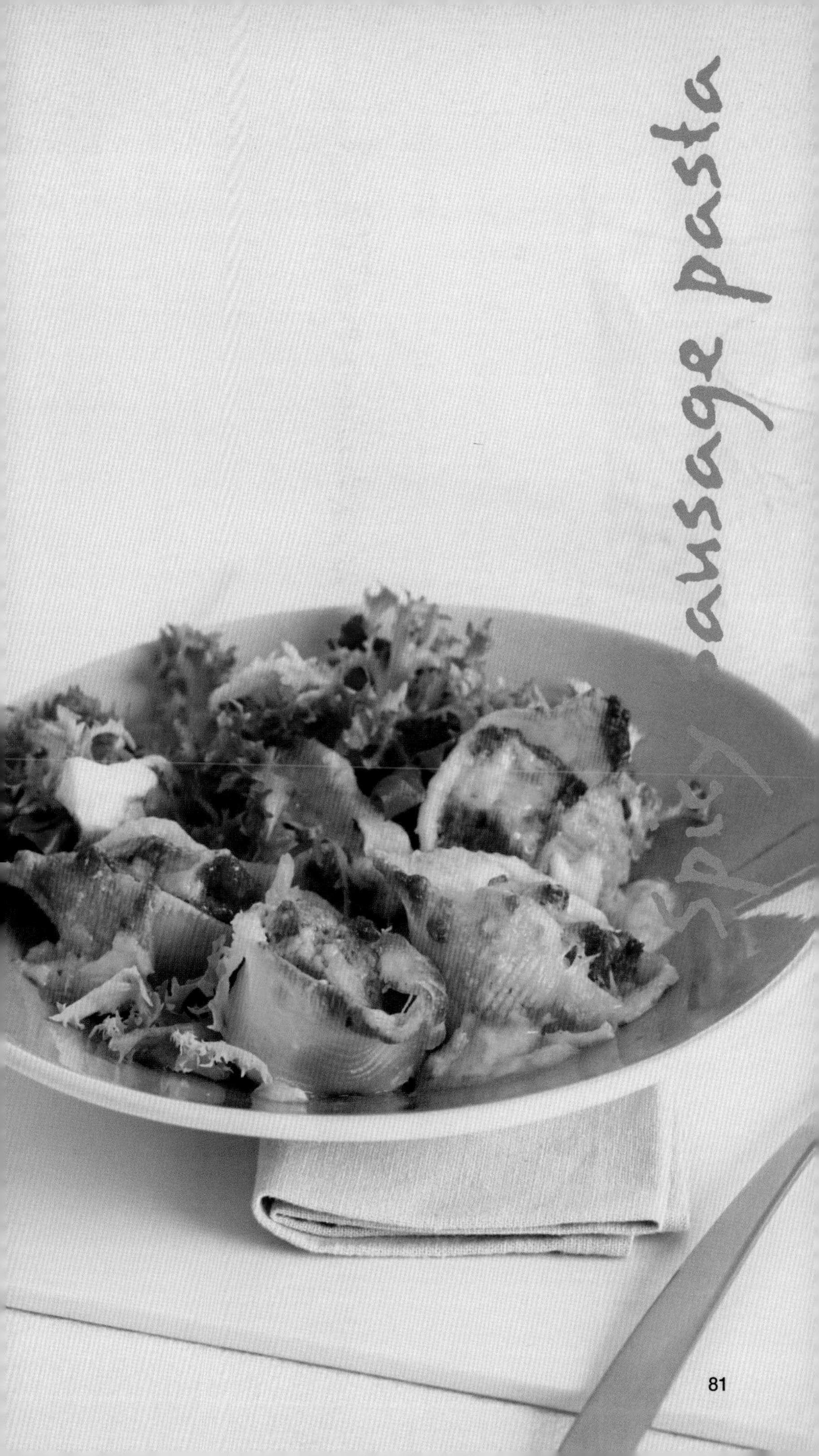

spicy sausage pasta

Pepperoni pizza waffles

Serves 4
Ready in 20 minutes

8 potato waffles

16–24 thin slices of
pepperoni

2 large tomatoes, sliced

100 g/4 oz mushrooms,
quartered

10 ml/2 tsp oil

150 g/5 oz Mozzarella
cheese, thinly sliced

1 Preheat the oven to 220°C/425°F/gas 7/
fan oven 200°C.

2 Place the waffles on a baking tray and cook
towards the top of the oven for 6 minutes,
turning them half-way through the cooking time.

3 Remove the waffles from the oven and top
with the pepperoni, placing two or three
slices on top of each. Top with the tomato slices
and mushrooms, then finish with the Mozzarella
slices.

4 Return the waffles to the oven and cook for
a further 8 minutes or until the cheese is
melted and bubbling.

Serve with
A mixed salad

Tip

- Potato waffles make a quick and easy
pizza base and are delicious with a
huge variety of toppings. Try
sweetcorn and tuna, or crispy bacon,
or make use of leftover vegetables
such as peppers and courgettes
(zucchini).

Pepperoni pizza waffles

Seafood

Delicious, healthy and versatile, seafood is a great source of protein and oily fish offers beneficial heart-healthy fats that are also said to be good for the brain! It's worth a try isn't it? When buying fish, remember that if it's really fresh it shouldn't smell 'fishy'. It's difficult to test pre-packed fish for freshness, but make sure it looks firm and moist. When you buy frozen seafood, make sure the packaging is undamaged and that there is little visible ice in the pack and no discolouration of the seafood. Fresh and frozen seafood should be put in the fridge or freezer as soon as possible and ideally fresh fish should be eaten on the day you buy it.

Speedy prawn linguine

Serves 4
Ready in 15 minutes

450 g/1 lb fresh linguine

30 ml/2 tbsp oil

1 garlic clove, peeled and crushed or finely chopped

225 g/8 oz cooked, peeled prawns (shrimp)

Finely grated zest and juice of 1 lime

1 bunch of fresh basil, roughly torn

Salt and freshly ground black pepper

Wedges of lime, to garnish (optional)

1 Cook the pasta in a large pan of boiling water for 8–10 minutes, or according to the packet instructions, until al dente (tender but firm to the bite). Drain in a colander and cover with the pan lid to keep it warm.

2 Heat the oil in the pan, add the garlic and cook for 1 minute. Add the prawns, lime zest and juice and mix well. Return the pasta to the pan and add the basil.

3 Gently toss the mixture over a low heat for about 1 minute, then season to taste with salt and pepper and serve straight away, garnished with lime wedges, if liked.

Tip

- Occasionally raw tiger prawns are on special offer or reduced for a quick sale (especially before bank holidays). Use them instead of ordinary prawns in this dish, adding with the garlic and stir-frying over a high heat for 2–3 minutes until pink and cooked through.

speedy prawn linguine

Herby rice and fish salad

Serves 4
Ready in 25 minutes

300 g/11 oz pack of fish fingers

225 g/8 oz/1 cup easy-cook long-grain rice

Salt and freshly ground black pepper

30 ml/2 tbsp oil

Juice of ½ lemon or 30 ml/ 2 tbsp bottled lemon juice

1 garlic clove, peeled and crushed or finely chopped, or 5 ml/1 tsp garlic purée (paste)

45 ml/3 tbsp chopped fresh herbs such as parsley, dill and chives

4 ripe tomatoes, quartered and roughly chopped

4 cornichons (gherkins), drained and chopped, or 30 ml/2 tbsp capers

1 Preheat the grill (broiler) to medium. Arrange the fish fingers on the grill rack and cook for 15 minutes until crisp and golden brown, turning them over half-way through the cooking time.

2 Meanwhile, cook the rice in plenty of boiling salted water for 10 minutes, or according to the packet instructions, until just tender.

3 Whisk together the oil, lemon juice, garlic, herbs and a little ground black pepper in a large bowl.

4 Drain the rice well, then add to the bowl and mix well. Stir the tomatoes and cornichons or capers into the rice.

5 Break the fish fingers into small pieces and stir into the rice. Serve straight away while the fish fingers are still crunchy.

Tips

- Don't buy cheap fish fingers. Choose white fish fillet fingers, then you'll know you are actually eating fish!

- This dish can be served warm or cold. If you want to make it ahead, keep the rice salad and fish fingers separate. Cover the rice with clingfilm (plastic wrap) and chill in the fridge for up to 6 hours. Add the fish finger pieces just before serving.

Salade niçoise

Serves 4
Ready in 30 minutes

3 hard-boiled (hard-cooked) eggs

225 g/8 oz green beans, halved if preferred

1 garlic clove, peeled and halved

4 Little Gem lettuces

½ cucumber, thinly sliced

225 g/8 oz plum tomatoes, quartered

1 red (bell) pepper, halved, seeded and sliced

1 red onion, peeled, halved and thinly sliced

200 g/7 oz/small can of tuna, drained and flaked into large chunks

50 g/2 oz stoned (pitted) black olives (about 12)

45 g/1¾ oz/very small can of anchovy fillets, drained and halved (optional)

For the dressing

5 ml/1 tsp Dijon mustard

60 ml/4 tbsp oil, preferably olive

Juice of ½ lemon or 30 ml/ 2 tbsp bottled lemon juice

Salt and freshly ground black pepper

1 Peel the eggs, then cut them into quarters.

2 Put the beans in a pan and pour boiling water over to cover. Bring back to the boil and simmer for 5 minutes. Drain and rinse under cold water to cool.

3 Rub the inside of a salad bowl with the cut sides of the garlic. Separate the lettuce leaves and use to line the bowl. Add the cooled beans, cucumber, tomatoes, sliced pepper, onion, tuna, olives and anchovy fillets, if using.

4 To make the dressing, whisk together the mustard, oil, lemon juice and salt and pepper to taste in a bowl or shake them in a screw-top jar. Drizzle over the salad just before serving.

Serve with
Crusty French bread

Tips

- **To hard-boil eggs, put them at room temperature in a pan with tepid water to cover. Bring to the boil, then reduce the heat and simmer for 7 minutes. Remove the eggs with a slotted spoon and place in a bowl of cold water (this helps to prevent a black ring forming around the yolk). Peel when cool enough to handle.**

- **If you have a food processor or blender, make this creamy anchovy dressing: put 3 of the anchovy fillets and a peeled garlic clove in the bowl and process to a purée. Add the mustard, oil and lemon juice and process until smooth.**

Salade niçoise

Tuna with peppers

Serves 4
Ready in 30 minutes

250 g/9 oz/generous 1 cup mixed basmati and wild rice, rinsed

Thinly pared zest and juice of 1 lime

Salt and freshly ground black pepper

4 tuna steaks, about 5 cm/2 in thick, about 400 g/14 oz total weight

30 ml/2 tbsp oil

3 small or 2 medium (bell) peppers, halved, seeded and sliced

60 ml/4 tbsp Thai sweet chilli sauce

1 Cook the rice with the lime zest in a pan of lightly salted boiling water for 20 minutes, or according to the packet instructions, until tender. Drain the rice and tip it into a bowl. Discard the lime zest.

2 When the rice has been cooking for about 12 minutes, brush the tuna steaks on both sides with half the oil and season with pepper. Heat a large non-stick frying pan or a ridged cast iron grill pan. Add the tuna steaks and cook over a moderately high heat for about 4 minutes on each side until lightly browned. Do not overcook or the tuna will be dry.

3 While the fish is cooking, heat the remaining oil in a non-stick frying pan, add the peppers and stir-fry for 4–5 minutes. Add the lime juice and sweet chilli sauce and cook for 1 minute.

4 Serve the tuna straight away with the sweet and spicy peppers and rice.

Tips

- If you have only one frying pan, cook the peppers first, then tip into a bowl. Wipe the pan clean with kitchen paper (paper towels) before cooking the fish. Serve the tuna, then quickly reheat the peppers for about 1 minute before serving.

- A bag of mixed peppers is relatively cheap and can be used in a variety of dishes including stir-fries, curries, omelettes and salads.

Crunchy fish fingers

Serves 4
Ready in 25 minutes

450 g/1 lb firm white fish,
skinned

2 eggs

45 ml/3 tbsp plain (all-
purpose) flour

Salt and freshly ground
black pepper

100 g/4 oz pack of plain or
soured (dairy sour) cream
and onion crisps, finely
crushed

Fresh chives and lemon
wedges, to garnish (optional)

1 Preheat the oven to 200°C/400°F/gas 6/ fan oven 180°C. Check the fish and remove any bones, then cut the flesh into strips measuring about 2 cm/¾ in x 7.5 cm/3 in.

2 Lightly beat the eggs on a shallow plate. Season the flour with salt and pepper on a second plate and put the crushed crisps on a third.

3 Dip the fish strips first in the seasoned flour, then the egg, then in the crisps to coat. Place on a non-stick baking tray, spacing them a little apart.

4 Bake in the oven for 10–12 minutes or until golden brown and cooked through, turning them over half-way through the cooking time.

5 Serve hot, garnished with chives and lemon wedges, if liked.

Serve with
A home-made or bought dip and oven chips (fries) or jacket potatoes (see page 17) and salad (see page 19)

Tips

- You'll find lots of ready-made dips in the supermarket, but if you prefer to make your own (which will be fresher and probably cheaper) simply mix together a few chopped fresh herbs, some seasoning and a small carton of soured (dairy sour) cream or Greek-style yoghurt.

- Ask for advice at the fish counter when buying fish; unsmoked haddock or cod are both good choices, but there are plenty of other inexpensive varieties such as coley available.

- For crunchy garlic fish fingers, use garlic salt instead of ordinary salt, or whisk a crushed clove of garlic with the egg.

Crunchy fish fingers

Seafood and noodle salad

Serves 4
Ready in 20 minutes

225 g/8 oz dried flat rice
(cellophane) noodles
or egg noodles

Finely grated zest and juice
of 1 lime

1 small red chilli, seeded
and finely chopped

5 ml/1 tsp caster (superfine)
sugar

15 ml/1 tbsp nam pla fish
sauce or soy sauce

2 ripe avocados

200 g/7 oz bag of mixed
salad leaves

400 g/14 oz bag of mixed
cooked seafood, thawed if
frozen

1 orange, peeled and
segmented

Fresh mint leaves, to garnish
(optional)

1 If using rice noodles, put them in a bowl and pour boiling water over. Soak for 3–4 minutes, then drain and rinse. If using egg noodles, cook them in a pan of boiling water for 3–4 minutes or according to the packet instructions. Drain thoroughly and leave in a bowl of cold water (this will stop them sticking together) until ready to use.

2 Put the lime zest and juice, chilli, sugar and nam pla or soy sauce in a large bowl and whisk together with a fork.

3 Cut the avocados in half around the stone (pit), then remove the stone and peel off the skins. Cut the flesh into thick slices, add to the dressing and toss to coat (this will stop the avocados turning brown).

4 Drain the noodles well, then pile on to four plates with the salad leaves. Add the seafood and orange segments to the avocado and gently mix together. Spoon on top of the noodle salad.

5 Garnish with a scattering of mint leaves, if liked, and serve straight away.

Tip

- You'll find mixed seafood at the fish counter or in the frozen fish section. The contents may vary, but will usually be a combination of prawns (shrimp), mussels and squid.

seafood and noodle salad

Spicy seafood pasta

**Serves 4
Ready in 15 minutes**

400 g/14 oz dried pasta
shapes such as shells or
quills

15 ml/1 tbsp oil

1 small onion, peeled and
finely chopped

2 garlic cloves, peeled and
crushed or very finely
chopped

400 g/14 oz/large can of
chopped tomatoes with chilli

400 g/14 oz bag of mixed
cooked seafood, thawed if
frozen

Salt and freshly ground
black pepper

15 ml/1 tbsp snipped fresh
chives, to garnish (optional)

1 Cook the pasta in a large pan of lightly salted boiling water for 10 minutes, or according to the packet instructions, until al dente (tender but firm to the bite).

2 Meanwhile, heat the oil in a pan, add the onion and cook for 6–7 minutes over a medium heat, stirring frequently, until soft and just starting to colour. Add the garlic and cook for a few seconds, then stir in the tomatoes and seafood. Season to taste with salt and pepper and simmer for 2 minutes.

3 Drain the pasta in a colander and return to the pan. Add the seafood sauce and gently toss together. Serve straight away in warmed bowls with a sprinkling of chives, if liked.

Tips

- Chopped tomatoes with added flavourings are an easy way to jazz up a sauce. They come with added fresh chopped chilli pepper (as used here) and herb and garlic varieties.

- You should be able to work out the weight of pasta from the packet size. If not, use a mug: a mugful of small pasta shapes weighs about 100 g/4 oz; a mugful of large pasta shapes about 50 g/2 oz.

seafood pasta

Thai prawn and veggie wraps

Serves 4
Ready in 15 minutes

60 ml/4 tbsp sweet chilli sauce

15 ml/1 tbsp soy sauce

225 g/8 oz cooked, peeled prawns (shrimp)

6 spring onions (scallions), finely sliced

1 large carrot, peeled and finely shredded

½ cucumber, peeled if preferred, and finely shredded

30 ml/2 tbsp chopped fresh coriander (cilantro)

4 x 20 cm/8 in wheat tortillas

Coriander or mint leaves, to garnish (optional)

1 Whisk together the chilli sauce and soy sauce in a bowl. Add the prawns, spring onions, carrot, cucumber and coriander and mix together well.

2 Warm the tortillas, one at a time, for just a few seconds in a dry frying pan. Divide the filling between them and roll up tightly. Cut each tortilla diagonally in half and garnish with coriander or mint leaves, if liked. Serve straight away.

Tips

- Substitute cooked shredded chicken for the prawns, if you prefer.

- Sweet chilli sauce is a thick sticky sauce made from red chillies and fresh and pickled garlic. You'll find it in the oriental foods section at the supermarket.

Thai prawn and veggie wraps

Grilled pepper and tuna salad

Serves 4
Ready in 30 minutes

3 large mixed coloured (bell)
peppers, halved and seeded

15 ml/1 tbsp oil

15 ml/1 tbsp fresh or bottled
lemon juice

1 garlic clove, peeled and
crushed or very finely
chopped

1 small red onion, peeled,
halved and thinly sliced

2 x 200 g/7 oz/small cans of
tuna, drained

30 ml/2 tbsp capers, rinsed
and drained

60 ml/4 tbsp chopped fresh
herbs such as chives and
parsley (optional)

Salt and freshly ground
black pepper

150 g/5 oz bag of rocket or
baby salad leaves

1 Place the peppers under a hot grill (broiler), skin sides up, for 10 minutes or until the skins are charred and blistered. Place them in a plastic bag and leave for 10 minutes (the steam will help soften the skins, making them easy to peel). Carefully remove the peel from the peppers, then cut the flesh into thick strips.

2 Whisk together the oil, lemon juice and garlic in a bowl, add the pepper strips and onion slices and mix well.

3 Flake the tuna into large chunks and add to the pepper mixture with the capers and herbs. Season with a little salt and pepper, then gently mix together, taking care not to break up the peppers or tuna flakes too much.

4 Divide the rocket or salad leaves between four serving plates or bowls, then top with the tuna and pepper salad. Serve straight away.

Tip

- Grilled peppers have a lovely smoky sweet flavour, so don't leave out this important step; it's well worth the effort. Look out for bags of mixed peppers; they usually work out a lot cheaper than buying individually. If they are on the small side, just use four instead of three large ones.

Grilled pepper and tuna salad

Prawn and rocket pasta

Serves 4
Ready in 25 minutes

350 g/12 oz dried pasta shapes

10 ml/2 tsp oil

2 garlic cloves, peeled and crushed or finely chopped

400 g/14 oz/large can of chopped tomatoes

120 ml/4 fl oz/½ cup vegetable stock

8 black olives

225 g/8 oz cooked and peeled large prawns (shrimp)

60 ml/4 tbsp chopped fresh basil leaves

50 g/2 oz rocket leaves

Salt and freshly ground black pepper

1 Cook the pasta in a large pan of boiling water for 10 minutes, or according to the packet instructions, until al dente (tender but firm to the bite).

2 Meanwhile, heat the oil in a saucepan, add the garlic and cook gently for a few seconds. Add the tomatoes and stock and simmer uncovered for 6–7 minutes.

3 Stir in the olives, prawns and basil and simmer for a further 1 minute to heat through.

4 Drain the pasta in a colander, then return to the pan. Add the rocket leaves and pour the tomato and prawn sauce over. Gently toss together, season with salt and pepper and serve straight away.

Tips

- If you are lucky enough to be given some home-grown plum tomatoes, or manage to buy some at a reasonable price on a fruit and vegetable stall, use 400 g/14 oz, quartered and seeded, instead of canned tomatoes.

- When raw tiger prawns are reasonably priced, buy them to make this dish really special. Add them to the sauce for the last 2–3 minutes of the cooking time, simmering until they are just cooked and pink.

prawn and rocket pasta

Mediterranean pizza

Serves 4
Ready in 30 minutes

1 plain or cheese-flavoured
foccacia loaf,
approx 18 cm/7 in diameter

90 ml/6 tbsp sun-dried
tomato paste

285 g/10½ oz jar of
artichokes in oil

1 red (bell) pepper, seeded
and sliced

1 yellow pepper, seeded and
sliced

Salt and freshly ground
black pepper

150 g/5 oz Mozzarella
cheese, thinly sliced

1 avocado, peeled and
sliced

25 g/1 oz/2 tbsp toasted
pine nuts

50 g/2 oz rocket or baby
salad leaves

1 Preheat the oven to 200°C/400°F/gas 6/fan oven 180°C. Cut the foccacia in half horizontally and place, cut-sides up, on a large baking (cookie) sheet. Spread the tomato paste thinly and evenly on top.

2 Drain the artichokes, reserving 15 ml/1 tbsp of the oil. Cut the artichokes into halves or quarters.

3 Put the pepper slices in a bowl, drizzle the artichoke oil over, season with salt and pepper, then gently toss together to coat.

4 Arrange the artichoke pieces and Mozzarella slices on top of the foccacia. Bake in the oven for 15 minutes or until the cheese is golden and bubbling.

5 Remove and cut each pizza in half to make four servings. Top with the avocado slices (if liked, you can put these on a hot griddle pan for a few minutes for a stripy charred effect), the pine nuts and salad leaves and serve straight away.

Tip

- If the avocado you've bought is slightly hard, put it in a brown paper bag with a banana for a day or so; this will speed up the ripening.

Mediterranean pizza

Vegetarian

If you don't eat meat, do make sure you're getting plenty of iron; non-meat sources include eggs, dried fruit such as apricots and fortified breakfast cereals. Chocolate also contains a reasonable amount of iron, but don't over-indulge! Eating or drinking vitamin-C rich foods, such as a glass of orange juice, with a meal will help the body to absorb iron, while drinking coffee or tea shortly before or after will prevent iron absorption. If you're a vegan, remember that pulses and beans are protein-packed, especially when teamed with grains. These main courses aren't just for vegetarians, though, and even the most avid meat-lover will find plenty to try.

Mixed vegetable biryani

Serves 4
Ready in 30 minutes

15 ml/1 tbsp oil

1 onion, peeled and chopped

1 garlic clove, peeled and crushed or finely chopped

100 g/4 oz button mushrooms, quartered

5 ml/1 tsp ground coriander (cilantro)

5 ml/1 tsp ground cumin

300 g/10 oz/1¼ cups basmati rice, rinsed

200 g/7 oz/small can of chopped tomatoes

400 ml/14 fl oz/1¾ cups hot vegetable stock

Salt and freshly ground black pepper

250 g/9 oz frozen mixed vegetables, thawed

15 ml/1 tbsp toasted flaked (slivered) almonds

1 Heat the oil in a large saucepan, add the onion and cook gently for 7–8 minutes until almost soft. Add the garlic, mushrooms and spices. Cook for a further 1 minute, stirring all the time, then stir in the rice.

2 Add the tomatoes and stock and season with salt and pepper to taste. Bring to the boil, reduce the heat, cover and simmer for 8 minutes.

3 Stir in the mixed vegetables, re-cover the pan and cook for a further 3–5 minutes or until the vegetables are tender and the rice is cooked and has absorbed the liquid. Leave to stand for a minute or two, sprinkle with the almonds and serve hot.

Serve with
Popadoms

Tips

- Uncooked popadoms can be cooked in the microwave. Allow 30 seconds for one and add an extra 10 seconds for each additional one.

- Almonds add extra protein to this vegetarian dish as well as a delicious crunchy texture. Use toasted cashew nuts for a change.

vegetable biryani

Vegetable stir-fry

Serves 4
Ready in 20 minutes

100 g/4 oz/1 cup cashew nuts

250 g/9 oz pack of medium egg noodles

30 ml/2 tbsp oil

50 g/2 oz trimmed green beans

125 g/5 oz pack of baby sweetcorn, halved lengthways

125 g/5 oz oyster or button mushrooms, sliced

200 g/7 oz pack of beansprouts

1 bunch of spring onions (scallions), sliced

1 garlic clove, peeled and crushed or finely chopped

1 red chilli, seeded and finely chopped, or 5 ml/1 tsp chilli purée (paste)

10 ml/2 tsp finely chopped fresh root ginger or ginger paste (purée)

1 Put the cashew nuts in a large non-stick frying pan and cook over a medium heat for 2–3 minutes or until golden brown. Remove from the pan and set aside.

2 Put the noodles in a pan and pour plenty of boiling water over. Bring back to the boil, then half-cover the pan with a lid and simmer for 2 minutes. Turn off the heat and leave the noodles for a further 3–4 minutes to cook in the residual heat.

3 While the noodles are cooking, make the stir-fry. Heat the oil in a large non-stick frying pan over a medium-high heat, add the beans, sweetcorn and mushrooms and stir-fry for 2 minutes.

4 Add the beansprouts and spring onions and cook for a further 2 minutes, then stir in the garlic, chilli and ginger and stir-fry for 1 more minute.

5 Drain the noodles in a colander, then add to the stir-fry and gently mix over a high heat for a few more seconds. Serve straight away, scattered with the toasted cashew nuts.

Serve with
Prawn crackers and soy sauce

Tips

- For an even faster stir-fry, or if you have only a one-ring hob, use 4 x 150 g/5 oz packs of straight-to-wok medium noodles.

- We should all be eating at least five portions of fruit and veg each day. They still count whether fresh, frozen, tinned, dried or juiced (but juice counts as only one portion per day, even if you drink more than one glass).

Vegetable stir-fry

Vegetable frittata

Serves 4
Ready in 40 minutes

30 ml/2 tbsp oil

1 onion, peeled and finely chopped

1 red (bell) pepper, halved, seeded and diced

1 garlic clove, peeled and crushed or finely chopped

350 g/12 oz cooked potatoes, peeled and diced

225 g/8 oz frozen peas, thawed

8 eggs

45 ml/3 tbsp chopped fresh herbs or 5 ml/1 tsp dried mixed herbs

Salt and freshly ground black pepper

30 ml/2 tbsp finely grated Parmesan cheese

1 Heat the oil in a large non-stick frying pan, add the onion and cook gently for 7–8 minutes until almost soft. Add the red pepper and cook for a further 3 minutes.

2 Turn up the heat a little, then add the garlic, potatoes and peas and stir-fry for a further minute. Spread out to an even layer on the base of the pan.

3 Beat the eggs in a bowl with the herbs and a little salt and pepper, then pour over the vegetables. Turn the heat to low, cover and cook gently for 10–12 minutes or until the base of the frittata is set and lightly browned.

4 Remove from the heat and place the frittata under a medium-hot grill (broiler). Cook for 4–5 minutes or until the top is set and golden brown. Remove from the heat and allow to cool in the pan for a few minutes before cutting into thick wedges. Sprinkle with the Parmesan cheese before serving.

Tips

- Plan ahead and cook extra potatoes the night before you make this dish – you'll need a couple of medium-sized ones.

- This dish is also a great way to use up leftover cooked vegetables; courgettes (zucchini), broccoli and carrots all work well.

vegetable frittata

Carrot and courgette pasta

Serves 4
Ready in 20 minutes

400 g/14 oz dried
pappardelle or tagliatelle

100 g/4 oz sugar snap peas
or mangetout (snow peas)

2 carrots, peeled

2 medium courgettes
(zucchini), trimmed

25 g/1 oz/2 tbsp butter or
sunflower margarine

2.5 cm/1 in piece of fresh
root ginger, peeled and
grated, or 10 ml/2 tsp ginger
purée (paste)

Salt and freshly ground
black pepper

15 ml/1 tbsp chopped fresh
parsley, to garnish (optional)

1 Cook the pasta in a large pan of lightly salted boiling water for 8–10 minutes or according to the packet instructions, adding the sugar snap peas or mangetout for the last 2 minutes of the cooking time.

2 Meanwhile, using a potato peeler, shave the carrots and courgettes into ribbons.

3 Melt the butter or margarine in a frying pan, add the carrots and courgettes and cook gently for 3 minutes. Add the ginger and cook for 2 more minutes or until everything is tender.

4 Drain the pasta and sugar snap peas or mangetout in a colander, then return to the pan. Add the carrot and courgette mixture and toss gently together. Season with salt and pepper to taste and serve straight away, sprinkled with parsley, if liked.

Tip

- For extra protein, serve with some grated or crumbled cheese to sprinkle over. This also makes a great accompaniment to grilled meat or fish.

caviar and courgette pasta

Stuffed roasted peppers

Serves 4
Ready in 30 minutes

4 large red (bell) peppers

225 g/8 oz Mozzarella cheese, diced

1 courgette (zucchini), trimmed and diced

12 cherry tomatoes, halved

60 ml/4 tbsp green pesto

Salt and freshly ground black pepper

1 Preheat the oven to 200°C/400°F/gas 6/fan oven 180°C. Halve the peppers lengthways and carefully remove the cores and seeds with a sharp knife. Place them cut-sides up on a baking tray.

2 Put the Mozzarella, courgette, tomatoes and pesto in a bowl and season with a little salt and pepper. Mix together well, then use to stuff the pepper halves.

3 Roast the peppers in the oven for 20 minutes or until they are tender and the cheese is golden and bubbling. Serve straight away.

Serve with
Boiled rice (see page 16) with some chopped fresh herbs, such as parsley, stirred into the rice

Tips

- Once opened, a jar of pesto will keep for about 6 weeks in the fridge. As well as the classic 'green' pesto made with basil, garlic, pine nuts, olive oil and Parmesan cheese, you can also buy 'red' pesto, which also contains sun-dried tomatoes.

- Always try to eat plenty of fruit and vegetables; they contain vitamins and minerals that are essential for good health.

Sweet potato stew

**Serves 4
Ready in 30 minutes**

15 ml/1 tbsp oil

1 onion, peeled and sliced

1 red (bell) pepper, halved, seeded and chopped

1 green pepper, halved, seeded and chopped

2 garlic cloves, peeled and crushed or finely chopped

15 ml/1 tbsp curry powder

900 g/2 lb sweet potatoes, peeled and cut into chunks

450 ml/¾ pint/2 cups hot vegetable stock

100 g/4 oz/5 tbsp crunchy peanut butter

Sprigs of fresh coriander (cilantro), to garnish (optional)

1 Heat the oil in a large pan over a medium heat, add the onion and cook for 6–7 minutes, stirring occasionally, until almost soft.

2 Add the red and green peppers, the garlic and curry powder and cook for 2 minutes, stirring all the time.

3 Stir in the sweet potatoes and stock and bring to the boil. Reduce the heat so that the mixture simmers gently, then cover and cook for 15 minutes.

4 Stir in the peanut butter and cook for a further 5 minutes or until all the vegetables are tender. Serve straight away, garnished with sprigs of fresh coriander, if liked.

Tip

- You could make up your own curry powder or paste to use in this recipe, if you prefer. It's best to buy the individual spices in small quantities – unless you eat a lot of curry – as they lose their flavour and pungency if kept too long.

sweet potato stew

Huevos rancheros

Serves 3 or 4
Ready in 25 minutes

15 ml/1 tbsp oil

1 onion, peeled and sliced

2 (bell) peppers of any colour, halved, seeded and sliced

2 garlic cloves, peeled and crushed or finely chopped

5 ml/1 tsp mild chilli powder

400 g/14 oz/large can of chopped tomatoes

3 or 4 eggs

Fresh coriander (cilantro) leaves, to garnish (optional)

1 Heat the oil in a large non-stick frying pan over a medium heat. Add the onion and cook for 6–7 minutes, stirring often, until beginning to soften.

2 Add the peppers and cook for 2 minutes, then add the garlic and chilli powder and cook for 1 minute.

3 Stir in the tomatoes and simmer for 5 minutes until slightly thickened. Turn the heat down to a really gentle simmer, then make 3 or 4 indentations in the sauce.

4 One at a time, break the eggs and gently place them in the indentations. Cover the pan with a lid and cook gently for 4–5 minutes or until the egg whites are set and the yolks cooked to your liking. Scatter some coriander leaves over, if liked, and serve straight away.

Tip

- Break each egg on to a saucer or small plate first. You can then check for any bits of shell before sliding them into the dents in the vegetable mixture.

huevos rancheros

Simple starters and snacks

Having friends round for a meal should be easy and fun, whatever the occasion. Being prepared before you start cooking can make all the difference. Adding a starter or finishing with a dessert – no matter how simple – makes a meal really special.

Choose a dish that can either be prepared ahead or is easy to put together at the last minute and plan a menu with a good range of tastes and textures. So, if you've chosen a rich, creamy pudding to finish with, don't serve a thick creamy soup as a starter – a light clear one would be better. Themed meals are fun! Try an Indian night, or French evening with bought pâté, Salade Niçoise (see page 88), followed by Crème Brûlée (see page 122).

Top tips
for great starters

The chill factor

Dips and dippers

- Buy an assortment or make your own! For guacamole, mash 2 ripe avocados with 30 ml/ 2 tbsp of fresh or bottled lemon juice, 1 peeled and crushed garlic clove and salt and freshly ground black pepper to taste. Serve with an assortment of raw vegetables such as fingers of carrots and (bell) peppers, tortilla chips and mini popadoms.

Minted melon

- Halve two kinds of ripe melon, such as an orange-fleshed cantaloupe or charentais and a green ogen or galia, and scoop out the seeds. Cut into thin wedges and remove the skins. Whisk together 5 ml/1 tsp of caster (superfine) sugar, 10 ml/ 2 tsp of red wine vinegar, 30 ml/ 2 tbsp of sunflower oil and 30 ml/2 tbsp of chopped mint. Drizzle over the melon, then garnish with fresh mint.

Greek theme

- Serve bought houmous and taramasalata and home-made tzaziki: finely chop half a cucumber and mix with 150 ml/¼ pint/⅔ cup of Greek-style yoghurt, 1 crushed garlic clove, 10 ml/2 tsp of mint sauce and salt and black pepper to taste. Serve with warmed pitta bread strips and marinated olives.

Crostini

- Cut the crusty ends off a baguette and discard, then cut the loaf into 2 cm/¾ in thick slices. Toast the slices on both sides. Top with bought fish or spreadable meat pâté or cream cheese and tiny slivers of smoked salmon trimmings.

Some like it hot

Super soup

- Cheat with soup. Buy 'fresh' soup in a carton and dress it up with a swirl of crème fraîche or yoghurt and a sprinkling of chopped fresh herbs.

Baked potato skins

- Scrub small baking potatoes, brush the skins with a little oil and sprinkle with salt. Bake in an oven preheated to 200°C/400°F/gas 6/fan oven 180°C for 1–1¼ hours or until tender. Cut in half lengthways and scoop out the flesh (save for topping a fish or shepherd's pie). Halve each piece lengthways again and place flesh-sides up on a baking tray. Brush with a little melted butter, then return to the oven for 12 minutes or until golden and crisp. Serve with soured (dairy sour) cream mixed with fresh chopped herbs or dips.

Chinese style

- Serve bought sesame toasts and mini vegetable spring rolls hot with sweet chilli or plum sauce for dipping. A great starter for an oriental meal or stir-fry.

Cheese straws

- Unroll a pack of ready-roll puff pastry (paste). Brush with milk and sprinkle with finely grated mature Cheddar cheese and a couple of pinches of ground paprika. Cut into strips about 10 cm/4 in long and 1 cm/½ in wide. Twist the sticks and place on a non-stick baking (cookie) sheet or one lined with baking parchment. Lightly press down the ends of the sticks. Bake at 200°C/400°F/gas 6/fan oven 180°C for 10–12 minutes or until lightly browned and crisp. Cool on the baking sheets for a few minutes, then serve warm.

Snack attack

Cheesy pasta

- Try cook-quick pasta sprinkled with some grated or thinly sliced cheese.

Fish-finger butties

- Grilled fish fingers between two slices of buttered bread, with salad leaves and mayonnaise.

Savoury croissants

- Split open a croissant, add one or two thin cheese slices and pop under a hot grill for a minute until melted. Add a slice of ham.

Eggy bread

- Whisk an egg with 15 ml/1 tbsp of milk and some salt and pepper. Cut sliced bread into squares or triangles, dip into the egg mixture, then fry in 30 ml/2 tbsp of hot oil for about 2 minutes on each side.

Mini pizzas

- Cut English muffins or baps in half horizontally and grill for a minute until crisp. Spread with tomato purée (paste), then top with salami slices and Mozzarella cheese. Grill for 1–2 minutes.

Desserts for dummies

Yoghurt and fresh fruit are an ideal healthy way to finish off a meal, but if you're entertaining or just fancy indulging in a more decadent dessert, try these quick and easy ideas.

They make the most of ready-made desserts or things you can pick up in the supermarket, which you can then easily transform into stylish desserts to impress your friends – or make yourself feel special. None of them takes much of your busy time or scarce money, so you can afford to treat yourself now and then. A little of what you fancy does you good, as they say!

Top tips

for decadent desserts

Simple desserts to make

Cheat's trifle

- Arrange some trifle sponges in a big serving bowl (glass is ideal to show off the layers), then moisten by sprinkling them with a few spoonfuls of fruit juice or liqueur if you have some. Top with lots of fruit; fresh raspberries or strawberries are ideal if they're cheap and in season, but drained canned fruit is fine. Spoon over a carton of custard, then top with whipped cream (if you use aerosol cream, add it at the last minute) and a sprinkling of sugar strands or, for a slightly more sophisticated finish, some toasted flaked (slivered) almonds.

Crème brûlée

- Put some fruit in the bottom of ramekin dishes (custard cups) or individual glasses. Top with Greek-style yoghurt, then sprinkle the tops with light or dark brown sugar. Leave in the fridge for an hour or two; the sugar will dissolve and make a delicious caramel-like topping.

Peach melba

- Drain a can of peach halves. Push a can of raspberries in syrup through a fine sieve (strainer) to make a sauce. Fill each peach half with a small scoop of ice-cream, then drizzle the sauce over and serve. You could use apricot halves instead of peaches.

Caramel bananas

- Melt 25 g/1 oz/2 tbsp of butter or sunflower margarine, 40 g/1½ oz/3 tbsp of light brown sugar and a dash of lemon juice in a frying pan. Simmer for a minute, then add peeled bananas, halved lengthways, and cook for a further minute or two until soft. Serve with ice-cream. You can also cook thickly sliced apples and pears in the same way.

Easy crumble

- Empty a large can of fruit into an ovenproof dish, adding a spoonful or two of the juice. Melt 50 g/2 oz/¼ cup of butter or margarine in a saucepan and stir in 15 ml/1 tbsp of light brown sugar and 2 crumbled Weetabix. Sprinkle over the fruit and bake at 200°C/400°F/gas 6/fan oven 180°C for 15 minutes.

Eton mess

- Mix together fresh fruit (raspberries or strawberries when in season are ideal), crumbled meringues and whipped cream and serve immediately.

Lemon tarts

- Fold together equal quantities of lemon curd and whipped cream. Use to fill bought sweet mini pastry (paste) cases or brandy snap baskets.

Easy ways to dress up bought desserts

Fruit salad

- Mix a couple of cans of fruit together to make a more interesting fruit salad mix. Add some fresh fruit, such as a chopped kiwi fruit or some seedless grapes, so it looks as if you've made some effort! Serve in wine glasses.

Chocolate chip rice pudding

- Heat up some canned rice pudding. Add some chocolate chips and stir for just a few seconds. Serve straight away.

Proper pastry

- If you serve a bought pastry (paste) dessert, just dredge a little icing sugar through a sieve over the top, then bring it to the table on a plate with a flourish; much more impressive than serving it straight from the box.

Cheat's chocolate mousse

- Turn out or scoop bought desserts such as crème caramel or chocolate mousse on to plates. Add a swirl of aerosol cream and some crumbled chocolate flake.

Cake and custard

- Cut bought cake such as gingerbread or fruity teacake into thick slices. Heat each slice in the microwave for 30 seconds, then serve warm with hot custard.

Ice-cream with fudge sauce

- Inexpensive plain vanilla ice-cream can be turned into a delicious dessert with a chocolatey fudge sauce. Try gently melting a Mars bar in a saucepan with 45 ml/3 tbsp of milk or 2 small chocolate fudge fingers with 30 ml/2 tbsp of milk. Serve the warm sauce over scoops of ice-cream just before serving.

Teatime treats

There are times when making a home-made cake is very therapeutic – and times when eating one is even more so! Plus this is your chance to really impress your friends and flatmates. There's no need to tell them how quick and simple these recipes really are. To give yourself a boost if you are fed up, to remind yourself of home if you are homesick or to encourage your revision efforts – all are good baking times!

All-in-one plain cake

Serves 6
Ready in 1 hour

100 g/4 oz/½ cup soft margarine

175 g/6 oz/¾ cup caster (superfine) sugar

175 g/6 oz/1½ cups self-raising flour

2 eggs, lightly beaten

60 ml/4 tbsp milk

5 ml/1 tsp vanilla essence (extract) (optional)

Icing (confectioners') or caster sugar, to decorate

1 Preheat the oven to 180°C/350°F/gas 4/fan oven 160°C. Lightly grease and line the base of an 18 cm/7 in round cake tin with baking parchment or greaseproof (waxed) paper.

2 Place all the ingredients in a large bowl and beat well for about 2 minutes until smooth and well mixed. Spoon and scrape into the prepared tin and level the surface with the back of the spoon.

3 Bake in the oven for 35–40 minutes or until the cake has shrunk a little from the sides of the tin and springs back when the top is lightly pressed with a finger. Remove from the oven and leave to cool on a wire rack. Dust the top with icing or caster sugar before serving.

Tip

- This mixture can also be used to make individual 'fairy' cakes or cupcakes. Divide it between 12 cake cases (cupcake papers). Place them in a bun tin – if you have one; otherwise simply put them on a baking tray – and bake at 190°C/375°F/gas 5/fan oven 170°C for 12–15 minutes until they are well risen and firm. Cool on a wire rack.

Easy chocolate cake

Serves 8
Ready in 1¾ hours

60 ml/4 tbsp cocoa
(unsweetened chocolate)
powder

60 ml/4 tbsp boiling water

A 225 g/8 oz tub of soft
margarine

225 g/8 oz/1 cup light soft
brown or caster (superfine)
sugar

4 eggs, lightly beaten

225 g/8 oz/2 cups self-
raising flour

For the icing (frosting)

150 g/5 oz/1¼ cups plain
chocolate chips

150 ml/¼ pint carton of
soured (dairy sour) cream

1 Preheat the oven to 180°C/350°F/gas 4/fan oven 160°C. Grease two 20 cm/8 in round cake tins and line the bases with a round of baking parchment or greaseproof (waxed) paper.

2 Put the cocoa powder in a large mixing bowl; sift through a sieve (strainer), if you have one, to make it easier to mix. Add the water and blend together.

3 Beat in the margarine and sugar, then add the eggs and flour (again through a sieve if you have one) and beat everything together for about 1 minute until well mixed. Spoon and scrape into the prepared tins and level the tops with the back of the spoon.

4 Bake the cakes in the oven for about 25 minutes. Gently press the tops with a finger; if the cakes are cooked, they will feel springy.

5 Remove from the oven and leave in the tins for about 5 minutes. Carefully run a knife around the edge to loosen, then turn out on to a wire rack. Leave to cool, then peel off the greaseproof paper.

6 While the cakes are cooling, make the icing. Put the chocolate chips in a heatproof bowl and add the soured cream. Heat about 2 cm/¾ in of water in a saucepan until it bubbles. Turn off the heat, place the bowl in the pan and stir the chocolate and cream until melted. Leave the icing to cool, then put in the fridge for about 1 hour to thicken, stirring every now and then.

7 Spread a little of the icing over the top of one of the cakes, then put the other cake on top. Spread the rest of the icing over the top and down the sides of the cake. Keep in the fridge until ready to serve.

Tips

- When you buy soft margarine, check that it's suitable for baking.

- A spare oven shelf is perfect for cooling cakes on instead of a wire rack.

Muffins

300 g/11 oz/2¾ cups plain (all-purpose) flour

10 ml/2 tsp baking powder

150 g/5 oz/¾ cup caster (superfine) sugar

A pinch of salt

250 ml/8 fl oz/1 cup milk

120 ml/4 fl oz/½ cup sunflower oil

1 egg, lightly beaten

5 ml/1 tsp vanilla essence (extract) (optional)

1 Preheat the oven to 190°C/375°F/gas 5/fan oven 170°C. for at least 5 minutes. Line a 12-cup muffin tin with paper cases (cupcake papers), or simply place the cases on a baking tray.

2 Put the flour (there's no need to sift it first), baking powder, sugar and salt in a mixing bowl and stir them together.

3 Mix together the milk, oil, egg and vanilla essence in a separate bowl or a jug.

4 Add the wet ingredients to the dry ingredients and stir together briefly; the mixture should still look lumpy with a few specks of dry flour showing.

5 Divide between the muffin cases and bake in the oven for 18–20 minutes or until risen and golden.

6 Cool in the muffin tin or on the baking tray for 5 minutes, then transfer to a wire rack. Serve warm or cool.

Variations

- Double chocolate muffins: Substitute 30 ml/45 tbsp of cocoa (unsweetened chocolate) powder for the same amount of flour and stir 100 g/4 oz/1 cup of white, milk or plain chocolate chips into the dry ingredients.

- Cappuccino muffins: Substitute 30 ml/45 ml of cocoa (unsweetened chocolate) powder for the same amount of flour. Blend 15 ml/1 tbsp of coffee powder or granules with 15 ml/1 tbsp of hot water and stir into the wet ingredients. Serve the muffins with a dusting of drinking chocolate (sweetened chocolate) powder and with whipped cream, if liked.

- Marmalade breakfast muffins: Leave out the vanilla essence and add 30 ml/2 tbsp of orange marmalade to the mixture. Use unsweetened orange juice instead of the milk.

- Mixed berry muffins: Add 100 g/ 4 oz each of fresh or frozen raspberries and blueberries to the wet ingredients. Dust the tops with icing (confectioners') sugar before serving.

- Fruity muffins: Stir in 75 g/3 oz/ ½ cup of chopped dried fruit such as pears or apricots, or vine fruits such as raisins or sultanas (golden raisins). Add 5 ml/1 tsp of ground cinnamon or mixed (apple pie) spice as well.

Index

Entries in *italics* are recipes